INTRODUCTORY LOGIC

FOR CHRISTIAN AND HOME SCHOOLS

ANSWER KEY

JAMES B. NANCE

&

DOUGLAS J. WILSON

canonpress
Moscow, Idaho

James B. Nance and Douglas J. Wilson, *Introductory Logic for Christian and Home Schools: Answer Key*
Fourth edition, revised and expanded.
©1990, 1992 by Douglas J. Wilson; ©1997, 2006 by James B. Nance and Douglas J. Wilson.

First edition 1990.
Second Edition 1992.
Third Edition, Revised and Expanded, 1997.

Published by Canon Press, P. O. Box 8729, Moscow, ID 83843
800–488–2034 | www.canonpress.com

08 09 10 11 12   9 8 7 6 5 4

Cover design by Paige Atwood. M. C. Escher's "Dewdrop" © 2006 The M. C. Escher Company-Holland. All rights reserved. www.mcescher.com

Printed in the United States of America.

ISBN-10:   1-59128-034-6
ISBN-13: 978-1-59128-034-7

CONTENTS

UNIT FOUR: ARGUMENTS IN NORMAL ENGLISH 93

UNIT FIVE: INFORMAL FALLACIES 129

UNIT ONE

TERMS AND DEFINITION

CONTENTS

✒ *EXERCISE 1*

I. Write lexical definitions of the words *child* and *adult* which show the relationship between them.

> Child: A person who has not yet gone through puberty
> Adult: A person who has gone through puberty

2. The word *grace* is an ambiguous word. Write two lexical definitions for the word *grace*, giving two of its different meanings.

> Grace: undeserved favor
> Grace: beauty of motion

3. Write a precising definition of the word *soon* to clarify the vagueness in the sentence "I will be home soon."

> By *soon* I mean "before dinner."

4. Invent a stipulative definition for the word *ploff*.

> A crime that was nearly committed, but not quite.

5. Write a persuasive definition of the word *television* from the point of view of a mother who thinks her children watch too much of it.

> A television is a one-eyed brain sucker.

6. Write a short, imaginary dialogue between two people having a verbal dispute about the word *believe*. Then introduce a third person who settles the dispute by presenting lexical definitions for the word which eliminates the ambiguity.

> Example:
>
> Smith: "Satan certainly believes in God."
> Jones: "No, if Satan believed in God he would be saved, for all who believe are saved."
> Johnson: "By 'believe' I think Smith means 'takes as real' but Jones means 'puts his trust in.'"

✒ EXERCISE 2

Explain the error or problem with each genus and species hierarchy shown.

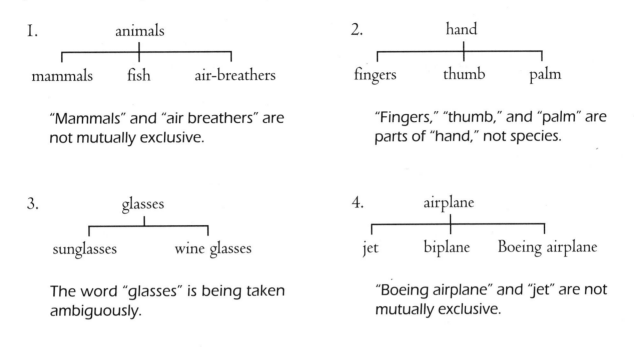

1.   animals

mammals   fish   air-breathers

"Mammals" and "air breathers" are
not mutually exclusive.

2.   hand

fingers   thumb   palm

"Fingers," "thumb," and "palm" are
parts of "hand," not species.

3.   glasses

sunglasses   wine glasses

The word "glasses" is being taken
ambiguously.

4.   airplane

jet   biplane   Boeing airplane

"Boeing airplane" and "jet" are not
mutually exclusive.

Fill in the genus and species hierarchy for each term given, identifying (a) a genus for the term,
(b) another species under that genus, and (c) a species of the term.

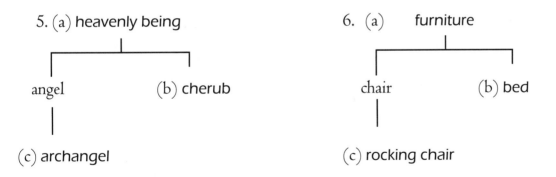

5. (a) heavenly being

angel   (b) cherub

(c) archangel

6. (a)   furniture

chair   (b) bed

(c) rocking chair

7. On the next page, draw a genus and species hierarchy which includes the following terms:
ALGEBRA, BIOLOGY, CHEMISTRY, GEOMETRY, MATH, PHYSICS, SCIENCE, SUBJECT

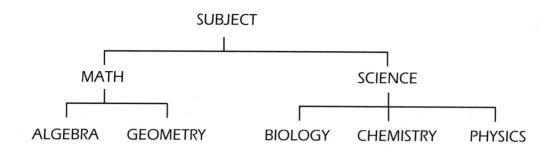

✒ *EXERCISE 3*

I. Arrange in order of increasing extension:
FIGURE, PLANE FIGURE, POLYGON, RECTANGLE, SQUARE

SQUARE, RECTANGLE, POLYGON, PLANE FIGURE, FIGURE

2. Arrange in order of decreasing extension:
INSTRUMENT, SCIMITAR, CURVED SWORD, SWORD, WEAPON

INSTRUMENT, WEAPON, SWORD, CURVED SWORD, SCIMITAR

3. Arrange in order of increasing intension:
ANCIENT LANGUAGE, CLASSICAL LATIN, COMMUNICATION, LANGUAGE, LATIN

COMMUNICATION, LANGUAGE, ANCIENT LANGUAGE, LATIN, CLASSICAL LATIN

4. Arrange in order of decreasing intension:
BAPTIST, CHRISTIAN, PROTESTANT, RELIGIOUS PERSON, SOUTHERN BAPTIST

SOUTHERN BAPTIST, BAPTIST, PROTESTANT, CHRISTIAN, RELIGIOUS PERSON

5. Determine the attribute or characteristic that distinguishes the term from the genus given in parentheses after the term.

TIMEPIECE (DEVICE): Designed to display the time of day.

CLOCK (TIMEPIECE): Other than a watch.

DIGITAL CLOCK (CLOCK): With a digital display.

✒ *EXERCISE 4*

Define the following terms by listing three examples of each.

I. *nation*	2. *board game*	3. *candy*
Japan	Monopoly	lollipop
Israel	Chess	chocolate bar
Egypt	Risk	licorice

Define these terms by identifying a synonym of each.

4. *happy:*   joyful

5. *job:*   occupation

6. *dinner:*   supper

Define the following words by genus and difference.

7. *brother:*   male sibling

8. *doe:*   female deer

9. *whisker:*   short facial hair

10. *queen:*   female monarch

11. *quiz:*   short test

12. *idol:*   false god

✒ EXERCISE 5

Identify the rule(s) broken by circling the correct number(s). Use the numbers in the following list: *A definition should* (1) *State the essential attributes of the term,* (2) *Not be circular,* (3) *Not be too broad or too narrow,* (4) *Not be unclear or figurative,* (5) *Not be negative when it can be positive,* and (6) *Be of the same part of speech as the term.*

DEFINITION	RULE #S BROKEN
1. *Mountain:* A natural object bigger than a hill.	1 2 ③ 4 5 6
2. *Wife:* Adam's rib.	① 2 3 ④ 5 6
3. *Brick:* Dried clay shaped into a brick.	1 ② 3 4 5 6
4. *Rectangle:* The shape of a typical textbook.	① 2 3 4 5 6
5. *Headache:* When your head hurts.	1 2 ③ 4 5 ⑥
6. *Capitalist:* A person who is not a socialist.	① 2 ③ 4 ⑤ 6
7. *To hate:* How you feel when you don't like something.	1 2 ③ 4 5 ⑥
8. *Carpet:* Floor covering.	1 2 ③ 4 5 6
9. *To float:* To hover.	1 ②③ 4 5 6
10. *Bag:* A pliant repository.	1 2 3 ④ 5 6
11. *Large:* Something that is not small.	1 2 3 4 ⑤⑥
12. *Life:* A roller coaster that we all ride.	① 2 3 ④ 5 6

Fill in the genus and species hierarchy for each term given, identifying a) a genus for the term, b) another species under that genus, and c) a species of the term.

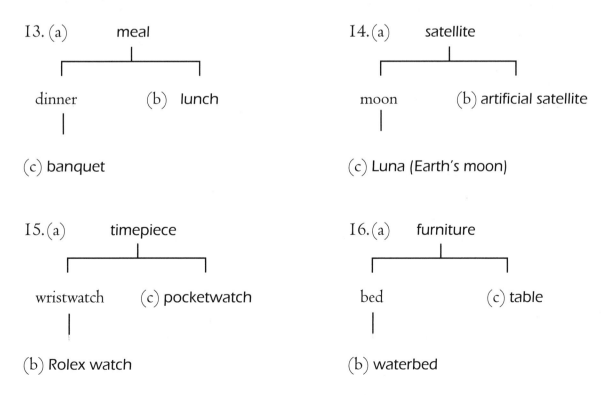

13. (a)   meal
    dinner   (b) lunch
    (c) banquet

14. (a)   satellite
    moon   (b) artificial satellite
    (c) Luna (Earth's moon)

15. (a)   timepiece
    wristwatch   (c) pocketwatch
    (b) Rolex watch

16. (a)   furniture
    bed   (c) table
    (b) waterbed

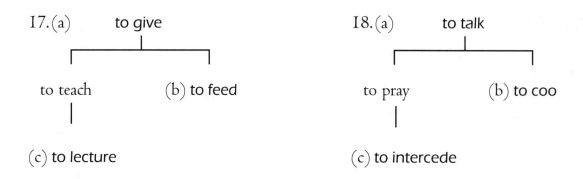

17. (a) to give
   to teach   (b) to feed
   (c) to lecture

18. (a) to talk
   to pray   (b) to coo
   (c) to intercede

Define the following terms by genus and difference, using the same genus from any corresponding terms in the charts above. Be careful not break any of the rules!

19. dinner: The main meal of the day

20. moon: A natural satellite

21. wristwatch: A timepiece worn on the wrist

22. bed: Furniture used for sleeping on

23. to teach: To give knowledge

24. to pray: To talk to God or a god

Answers to Selected Unit 1 Review Exercises

✒ *ADDITIONAL EXERCISES FOR LESSON 1*

1. Write (or find) lexical definitions for the following pairs of words which will show the relationship between them. Explain the relationship: How are the words similar? How are they different? Word pairs: *Brother/Sister, Breakfast/Dinner, Newspaper/Magazine, Circle/Sphere, Blind/Deaf, Huge/Tiny, To punch/To slap, To walk/To run.*

   Examples:

   Brother: Male sibling. *Sister:* Female sibling. The definitions show that the terms comprise the two genders for siblings.

   Circle: A plane figure consisting of the set of points at a given distance from the center. *Sphere:* A solid figure consisting of the set of points at a given distance from the center. The definitions show that both terms are figures made up of the set of points at a given distance from the center. The circle is a plane figure, but the sphere is a solid figure.

In questions 2–5, identify the type of definition used for the underlined word in the paragraph.

2. Consider the following description of Noah's ark: "Noah's ark was <u>big</u>. What do I mean by big, you ask? Well, the ark had a volume of about one and a half million cubic feet!"

   Precising definition

3. Rabbits were introduced to a small, populated island where they had no natural predators, and they rapidly overran the town there. In a letter to the editor, one citizen argued for their elimination, saying that "a <u>rabbit</u> is just a fuzzy rat!"

   Persuasive definition

4. In the book *The Structure of Scientific Revolutions*, the author Thomas Kuhn writes, "In this essay, '<u>normal science</u>' means research firmly based upon one or more past scientific achievements, achievements that some particular scientific community acknowledges for a time as supplying the foundation for its further practice."

   Stipulative definition.

5. In an editorial to the *London Times* titled "What is Relativity?" (November 28, 1919), Albert Einstein wrote, "The most important upshot of the special theory of relativity concerned the inert mass of corporeal systems. It turned out that the inertia of a system necessarily depends upon its energy-content, and this led straight to the notion that <u>inert mass</u> is simply latent energy."

Theoretical definition.

6. Read the short story "The Most Dangerous Game" by Richard Connell (if you do not have a copy, you may be able to find it on the Internet). In the title, the word *game* is purposely ambiguous. Write your own lexical definitions for both of the meanings of this word.

Game: (1) A recreational activity comprised of a set of rules which distinguish winning from losing; or (2) An animal hunted for sport.

7. Consider the following ambiguous words. How many different meanings or definitions (including different parts of speech) can you think of for each? Can you think of any other words that have multiple, distinct meanings? Words: *age, check, class, date, face, fair, fine, head, light, mean, point, race, round, scale, top.*

Each of these terms has at least three distinct meanings. For example,

Age: Length of life; Division of geological time; To become older.
Check: Exposure of a chess king to attack; Sudden stoppage of forward progress; Written order directing a bank to pay money; A mark (✓) placed beside an item to show it has been noted; To examine.

8. Can you think of some words that have only *one* meaning?

Examples: Aardvark, captor, centimeter, enrage, hexagon, joist, misspell, plywood, quiche, shale, titanium, urban.

✒ ADDITIONAL EXERCISES FOR LESSON 2

1. Explain how the words *genus* and *species* are related to the words *general* and *specific*.

A genus is a more *general* term in which the given term is included (the plural being *genera*). A species is a more *specific* term included in the given term. The terms have the same etymology, from the Latin.

2. Create genus and species charts for the following terms. Include at least a genus for the given term, another species under that genus, and two species for the given term. Terms: *coin, hero, monarch, piano, soldier, tree, truck, to drink, to kill.*

For example:

```
        Money                          Mythological figure
    ┌─────┴─────┐                      ┌────────┴────────┐
  Coin         Bill                  Hero             Titan
┌───┴───┐                             │                 │
Nickel  Dime                      Hercules         Prometheus
```

3. Consider the examples of proper genus and species charts in Lesson 2 and Exercise 2. Expand these charts by (1) introducing a new, higher genus, (2) introducing new, lower species, and (3) including more species to broaden the chart.

Example: From Exercise 2, problem 5.

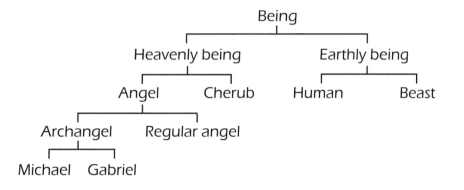

```
                              Being
                 ┌──────────────┴──────────────┐
          Heavenly being                  Earthly being
        ┌───────┴───────┐               ┌──────┴──────┐
     Angel           Cherub           Human         Beast
  ┌────┴────┐
Archangel  Regular angel
┌───┴───┐
Michael  Gabriel
```

4. In a genus and species chart, different species may be produced for a given term depending on the dividing principle being used (as the species of logic could be *formal* and *informal*, or *art* and *science*). For each of the given terms, produce two sets of species, and identify what dividing principle you are using. Terms: *water, computer, to talk.*

For example:

```
       Water                       Water
    ┌────┴────┐              ┌────────┴────────┐
  Ice      Steam         Saltwater        Fresh water
```

5. Complete a genus and species chart which includes the following terms: *Book of the Bible, Epistle, Genesis, Gospel, Hebrews, Jonah, Luke, Matthew, New Testament book, Romans.* Which term or terms did you need to introduce to complete this chart? Do the terms at a given level "line up" properly?

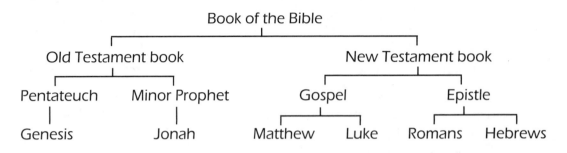

Needed to introduce "Old Testament book," "Pentateuch," and "Minor Prophet" to make the terms "Genesis" and "Jonah" line up with the other individual books.

✒ ADDITIONAL EXERCISES FOR LESSON 3

1. Arrange these terms in order of increasing extension: *banquet, dinner, formal dinner, meal, wedding banquet.*

   Wedding banquet, banquet, formal dinner, dinner, meal

2. Arrange these terms in order of increasing intension: *brother, child, human, sibling, twin brother.*

   Human, child, sibling, brother, twin brother

3. Arrange these terms in order of decreasing extension: *airplane, fighter, jet, F-14, vehicle.*

   Vehicle, airplane, jet, fighter, F-14

4. Arrange these terms in order of decreasing intension: *body, celestial body, gas giant, Jupiter, planet.*

   Jupiter, gas giant, planet, celestial body, body

5. Consider the term *gas giant* from the above list. Would adding the adjective *ringed* (i.e., *ringed gas giant*) change the extension? Would it change the intension?

   The extension would be unchanged, since all gas giants are ringed. The intension would increase.

6. For each of the following, determine the attribute or characteristic which distinguishes the term from the genus of the term given in parentheses: *term (word), idol (god), whisker (hair), fang (tooth), nightmare (dream), to accelerate (to move).*

    Term (word): Having a single, precise meaning
    Idol (god): False
    Whisker (hair): Of the beard
    Fang (tooth): Long, sharp
    Nightmare (dream): Frightening
    To accelerate (to move): Faster

7. Consider the second chapter of the epistle of James. What distinguishes *saving faith* from mere *belief*?

    Saving faith is belief which is alive and always results in good works.

8. Develop a list of four verbs arranged in order of increasing intension.

    To take in, to swallow, to drink, to drink wine

✒ *ADDITIONAL EXERCISES FOR LESSON 4*

1. Define each of the following terms by synonym, example, and genus and difference. Limit your synonyms to only one word, and include a variety when defining by example. Terms: *father, ghost, house, human, monarchy, hoop.*

    For example:

    Father. Synonym: Dad. Example: Abel's father was Adam, Charlie Sheen's father is Martin Sheen, John Quincy Adams' father was John Adams. Genus and difference: Male parent.

    Ghost. Synonym: Spirit. Example: Marley's ghost, Casper, the spirit of Samuel. Genus and difference: The soul of a dead person.

2. Another common method of defining terms is by etymology, in which the original language root of the word is used to clarify the meaning. For example, *monarchy* comes from the Greek *mon + arche,* meaning "one ruler." Define the following terms by etymology: *architect, manuscript, peninsula, submarine, telegram, translucent.*

    Architect: Greek *archi + tekton,* meaning "chief builder"

Manuscript: Latin *manus + scriptus*, meaning "thing written by hand"
Peninsula: Latin *paene + insula*, meaning "almost an island"
Submarine: Latin *sub + marinus*, meaning "under the sea"
Telegram: Greek *tele + gramma*, meaning "distant letter"
Translucent: Latin *trans + lucere*, meaning "to shine through"

✒ ADDITIONAL EXERCISES FOR LESSON 5

1. What is the primary rule broken by each of the following definitions?

Chair: a four-legged piece of furniture.	Too broad / Too narrow
Chess: a game played on a checkered board.	Too broad
Chick: juvenile poultry.	Unclear (obscure)
Salad: not a main dish and not a dessert.	Negative
To shake: a rapid back and forth motion.	Wrong part of speech
To think: to think about something.	Circular
Variety: the spice of life.	Figurative
Wood: hard material often burned in fireplaces.	Not essential attributes

2. Write proper genus and difference definitions for the following terms: *chair, coin, to drink, pebble, salad, to snore, to throw, wood, year.*

Chair: A piece of furniture made to seat one person
Coin: Metal money
To drink: To swallow liquid
Pebble: A small stone, usually rounded as in a stream
Salad: A dish usually consisting of leafy green vegetables and served with dressing
To snore: To breath audibly through the nose, usually while sleeping
To throw: To propel through the air
Wood: Hard substance making up the trunk or branches of trees
Year: The time for one complete orbit around the sun

3. The following terms are rather "negative." Write genus and difference definitions for each of them. Can you define them positively? Terms: *absence, death, empty, ignorance, infinite, sin.*

Absence: Lack of presence
Death: Loss of life
Empty: Containing nothing
Ignorance: Lack of knowledge
Infinite: Great beyond measure, without bounds
Sin: Lack of conformity unto or transgression of the law of God

4. Consider the "Do Re Mi" song from the movie *The Sound of Music*. If the definitions given in the song were considered serious, which would be good definitions by genus and difference? Of those which would be improper definitions, which rules are broken?

    Do (doe): "A female deer." This is a good definition.
    Re (ray): "A drop of golden sun." This is understandably figurative.
    Me: "A name I call myself." This seems an acceptable definition.
    Fa (far): "A long, long way to run." This is the wrong part of speech.
    So (sew): "A needle pulling thread." Also the wrong part of speech.
    La: "A note to follow 'so.'" Perhaps not very imaginative (why not "law: a rule that says 'No!'"?), but acceptable.
    Ti (tea): "A drink with jam and bread." Does not state the essential attributes.

5. Read the children's book *A Hole is to Dig*. What primary rule is broken by most of the definitions in that book?

    The definitions are usually the wrong part of speech: verbs for nouns.

6. In Galatians 5:22–23, Paul lists the fruit of the Spirit. Do the terms have a common genus? Write a genus and difference definition of each term which clarifies the distinctions between them.

    These are all Christian virtues, which may be used as a genus.
    Love: The virtue by which one gives himself for the good of another
    Joy: The virtue by which one delights in God's goodness
    Peace: The virtue by which one maintains a state of tranquility and harmonious relationships with others
    Patience: The virtue by which one bears trials without complaint
    Kindness: The virtue by which one serves others with a sweet disposition
    Goodness: The virtue by which one treats others in accordance to God's law
    Faithfulness: The virtue by which one does what he has promised to do
    Gentleness: The virtue by which one remains free from harshness
    Self-control: The virtue by which one governs one's passions

7. Can *God* be defined by a genus and difference definition? Consider the answer to question 4 in the Westminster Shorter Catechism, "What is God?": "God is a Spirit, infinite, eternal, and unchangeable, in his being, wisdom, power, holiness, justice, goodness, and truth." Compare this to how the Bible defines or describes God.

    One concern with a genus and difference definition of God is that, in one sense, there is no higher genus than God. The catechism answer does use a biblical genus, Spirit (John 4:24, 2 Cor. 3:17), but God's Spirit is divine, unlike all other spirits, which are created. To define or describe God, the Bible often uses metaphor (Exod. 15:2-3; Deut. 4:24; 2 Sam. 22:2-4, 29; Ps. 23:1; Is. 33:22, 63:16; 1 Jn. 1:5; Rev. 1:8), while glorifying God for who He is and what He has done.

UNIT TWO

STATEMENTS AND THEIR RELATIONSHIPS

CONTENTS

✒ EXERCISE 6

Examine the following sentences and determine whether or not they are statements. In the space provided, write down *true statement, false statement, question, command,* or *nonsense.* Be careful.

1. Jesus healed blind men.	True statement
2. King David was the first king of Israel.	False statement
3. The tongues of flame at Pentecost were water.	False statement
4. Who wrote the book of Hebrews?	Question
5. Children, obey your parents.	Command
6. The Bible is the Word of God.	True statement
7. The Great Pyramid is six feet high.	False statement
8. Who said slaves should obey their masters?	Question
9. How old was Jesus when He was baptized?	Question
10. The slithy toves did gyre and gimble.	Nonsense
11. Believe the good news.	Command
12. The United States has fifty states.	True statement

Challenge: Write a nonsense sentence which uses correct grammar.

Example: The flip will squirt a cruise yesterday in the bright despair.

🖊 *EXERCISE 7*

1. List below five examples of a phrase which would introduce a self-report, such as, "It is my opinion that . . ."

    I think . . .
    I believe . . .
    I feel that . . .
    I want . . .
    I know . . .

2. List below five statements of your own which are true or false by logical structure. Include at least one tautology and one self-contradiction.

    The sun is shining and it is not.
    I will go to school and I will not.
    You either eat or you do not eat.
    The coin will come up heads or not heads.
    A man can take a joke or he cannot take a joke.

3. List below five statements which are true or false by definition. Include at least one true statement and one false statement.

    Bachelors are unmarried.
    Bachelors are little girls.
    This square is four-sided.
    This square is not a polygon.
    Your uncle is your relative.

✒ EXERCISE 8

Examine each of the following statements. In the blank at the right, enter the type of statement you believe it to be. Your options are *self-report, tautology, self-contradiction, true* or *false by definition,* and *supported.*

1. The snow is deep.	Supported
2. I think Socrates was a wise man.	Self-report
3. Paul was an apostle, and he wasn't.	Self-contradiction
4. Jericho fell to the invading Israelites.	Supported
5. I believe Paris really loved Helen.	Self-report
6. A square has five sides.	False by definition
7. The book of Genesis has fifty chapters.	Supported
8. Jesus is God, or He is not God.	Tautology
9. Jesus is God, and He is man.	Supported
10. I think the snow is deeper than last year.	Self-report
11. Jeremiah was a reluctant prophet.	Supported
12. My mother is a woman.	True by definition
13. It either works, or it doesn't.	Tautology
14. Dante was a poet.	Supported
15. The New Testament was written in Greek.	Supported

✒ EXERCISE 9

With the following five sets of statements, circle Y if the statements are consistent, and circle N if they are not consistent.

1. The sun is hot.
   The moon is white.   (Y) N

2. Paul was the author of Romans.
   Peter was the author of Romans.   Y (N)

3. Sally told a lie once.
   Sally usually tells the truth.   (Y) N

4. All fish have fins.
   Some fish do not have fins.   Y (N)

5. God knows all things.
   God does not know all things.   Y (N)

For the next five sets of statements, circle Y if the first sentence implies the second, and circle N if it does not.

6. God created everything.
   God created porcupines.   (Y) N

7. All watermelons are green.
   Some watermelons are green.   (Y) N

8. Honey is sweet.
   I hate honey.   Y (N)

9. The Bible is the Word of God.
   Ecclesiastes is the Word of God.   (Y) N

10. Some trees are tall.
    All trees are tall.   Y (N)

Now seek to determine whether the statements in these sets are logically equivalent. If they are equivalent, circle Y; if not, circle N.

11. No Baptists are Americans.
    No Americans are Baptists.   (Y) N

12. All dogs are four-legged animals.
    All four-legged animals are dogs.   Y (N)

13. No apples are oranges.
    No oranges are bananas.   Y (N)

14. Some apostles were Scripture-writers.
    Some Scripture-writers were apostles.   (Y) N

15. No windmills are giants.
    No giants are windmills.   (Y) N

Lastly, examine these sets to determine independency. Circle Y if the statements are independent; circle N if they are not independent.

16. The typewriter is broken.
    Obadiah is my favorite book.   (Y) N

17. Logic is hard.
    Spanish is hard.   (Y) N

18. God created all the stars.
    God created this star.   Y (N)

19. Some triangles are yellow.
    Some tricycles are red.   (Y) N

20. Alan wrote this poem.
    Alan has written no poems.   Y (N)

Challenge: Consider these two statements: *Some soldiers are painters. Some soldiers are not painters.* Answer the following questions, explaining your answers.

Are these statements consistent?

   They are consistent, because they can both be true.

Does the first imply the second?

   The first does not imply the second. If it were true that some soldiers are painters, it would still be possible that all soldiers are painters.

Are they equivalent?

   They are not equivalent, because they can have different truth values.

Are they independent?

   They are not independent, because they cannot both be false.

✎ EXERCISE 10

Give examples of the three types of disagreements. (Even if the names are historical, your answers need not be.)

Real disagreement

1. Luther: No man has free will.

    Erasmus: All men have free will.

2. Lee: The South had the right to secede.

    Grant: The South did not have the right to secede.

Apparent disagreement

3. Peter: I think you should stay in Jerusalem.

    Paul: I think I should go to Rome.

4. Homer: I enjoy poetry that is sung.

    Virgil: I enjoy poetry that is recited.

Verbal disagreement (underline the word being defined differently)

5. William: All of <u>Scotland</u> must go to war.

    Robert: No, only the men of <u>Scotland</u> must go to war.

6. Write two statements which are consistent but not independent.

    All roads lead to Rome.
    At least some roads lead to Rome.

✒ EXERCISE 11

Rewrite each sentence using no verbs but the verb of being.

1. John eats turnips.

   John is a turnip eater.

2. Rebekah reads her Bible daily.

   Rebekah is a daily Bible reader.

3. Paul resisted Peter and Barnabas.

   Paul was a Peter and Barnabas resister.

4. Susan works hard to resist temptation.

   Susan is a person who works hard to resist temptation.

5. Faith produces fruit.

   Faith is a fruit producer.

6. The works of the sinful nature lead to death.

   The works of the sinful nature are to death leaders.

7. The donkey rebuked the prophet.

   The donkey was a prophet rebuker.

8. The man will sing loudly.

   The man will be a loud singer.

9. Absalom rebelled against King David.

   Absalom was an against-King-David rebel.

10. God created heaven and earth.

God is the Creator of heaven and earth.

✒ EXERCISE 12

In the following exercise, analyze each statement. In the blank at the right, put down what sort of categorical statement it is, i.e., universal affirmative, universal negative, particular affirmative, or particular negative.

1. Some cowboys are intellectuals.	Particular affirmative
2. All Scripture is God-breathed writing.	Universal affirmative
3. Some children are not students.	Particular negative
4. No Christians are Hindus.	Universal negative
5. Some books are fiction.	Particular affirmative
6. Some writers are not poets.	Particular negative
7. All dogs are carnivores.	Universal affirmative
8. No Trojans are Greeks.	Universal negative
9. Some soldiers are not brave men.	Particular negative
10. All men are mortal.	Universal affirmative

Translate the following sentences into one of the four standard forms.

11. Christians will not be condemned.

> No Christians will be condemned people.

12. Every false teacher attacks the authority of Scripture.

> All false teachers are authority-of-Scripture attackers.

(Continued on next page)

13. A few churches allow divorce too easily.

Some churches are too-easy divorce allowers.

14. Many people do not believe in the devil.

Some people are not believers in the devil.

✒ *EXERCISE 13*

Draw six squares of opposition using the instructions provided.

1. Place the four categorical statements at each corner, using the abbreviations *S* and *P*.

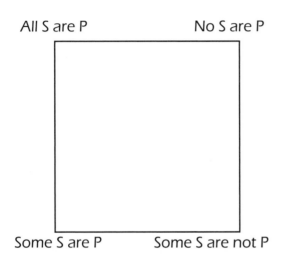

2. Place A, E, I or O at the appropriate corner.

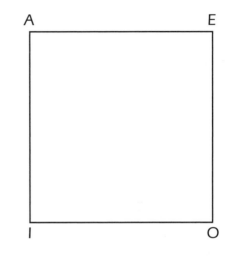

3. Enter the letters again, and draw in the appropriate lines of contradiction.

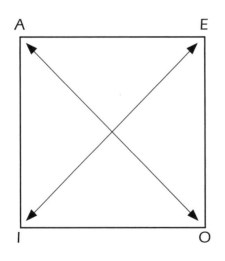

4. Use *dogs* as the subject and *cats* as the predicate (so the upper left-hand corner of the square would say *All dogs are cats*).

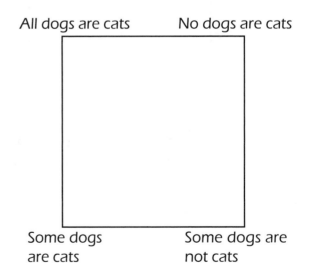

For the last two squares, make up categorical statements of your own and place them in the appropriate corners, making sure that for each square the four statements have the same subject and the same predicate.

5.

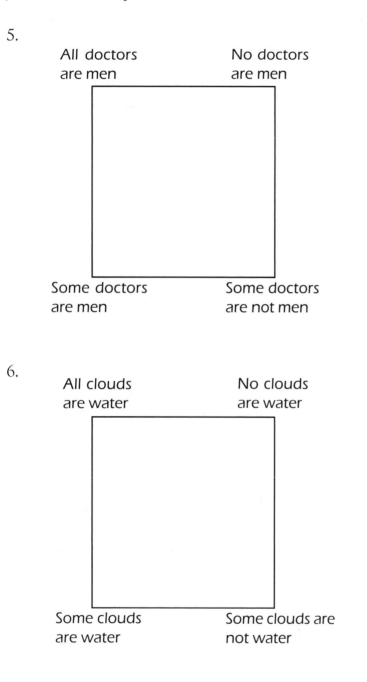

All doctors
are men

No doctors
are men

Some doctors
are men

Some doctors
are not men

6.

All clouds
are water

No clouds
are water

Some clouds
are water

Some clouds are
not water

✒ EXERCISE 14

Analyze the following arguments. Each of them contains two contradictory statements. Isolate those statements (ignoring the others), translate them into categorical statements with the same subject and predicate, and diagram where they are located on the square of opposition. Show all your work.

1. All logic students can see the problem here. However, some of them cannot see the problem (but they might if they think about it).

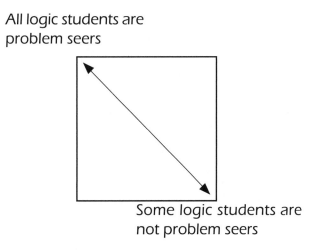

All logic students are
problem seers

Some logic students are
not problem seers

2. There is no good reason to believe that the Bible is the Word of God; it is simply the word of men. I admit that prophecies which were fulfilled is one good reason to believe it, though I am still unconvinced.

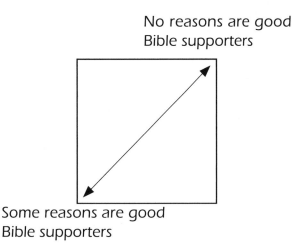

No reasons are good
Bible supporters

Some reasons are good
Bible supporters

✒ EXERCISE 15

Analyze the following paragraphs, isolate the related statements, and put them into categorical form. Assign abbreviations to the terms, place them on the square of opposition, and determine their relationship. One will show the relationship of contradiction, one the relationship of contrariety, and one subcontrariety. Show your work.

1. Johnny sneered at Billy, "All third-graders are stupid!" Billy shouted back, ineffectively countering Johnny's point, "That's not true! None of them are!"

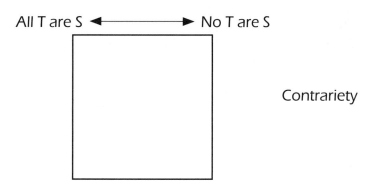

Contrariety

2. Smith said, "Pro-lifers don't care about children who are already born. All they care about is their stupid political agenda." Jones disagreed by saying, "No, there are many pro-lifers who are involved in caring for children."

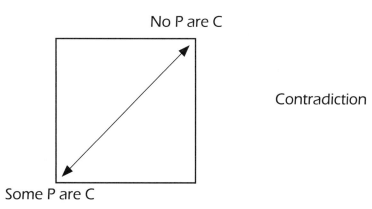

Contradiction

3. Some people I know are always complaining about their jobs; they never seem to quit. Of course, not everyone complains.

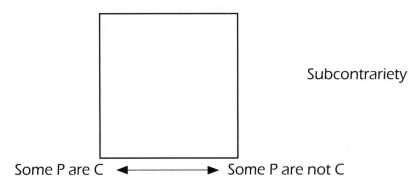

✒ *EXERCISE 16*

In the following exercise, write the relationship which exists between the two given statements in the blank at right. Their order does matter.

1. All cowboys are rough men.
    Some cowboys are not rough men.   Contradiction

2. Some ladies are not rude women.
    No ladies are rude women.   Superimplication

3. All Christians are forgiven sinners.
    Some Christians are forgiven sinners.   Subimplication

4. No Christians are Muslims.
    Some Christians are not Muslims.   Subimplication

5. All french fries are greasy food.
    No french fries are greasy food.   Contrariety

6. Some pictures are beautiful art.
    Some pictures are not beautiful art.   Subcontrariety

7. Some atheists are irrational men.
    No atheists are irrational men.   Contradiction

8. All eighth graders are brilliant logicians.
    Some eighth graders are brilliant logicians.   Subimplication

9. All violinists are right-handed players.
    Some violinists are not right-handed players.   Contradiction

10. Some feminists are feminine.
    All feminists are feminine.   Superimplication

11. All Democrats are Republicans.
    Some Democrats are not Republicans.   Contradiction

12. All bards are story-tellers.
    Some bards are story-tellers.   Subimplication

✒ EXERCISE 17

I. Draw the square of opposition, including all the arrows and relationships Include the abbreviated categorical statements in the corners, using S and P.

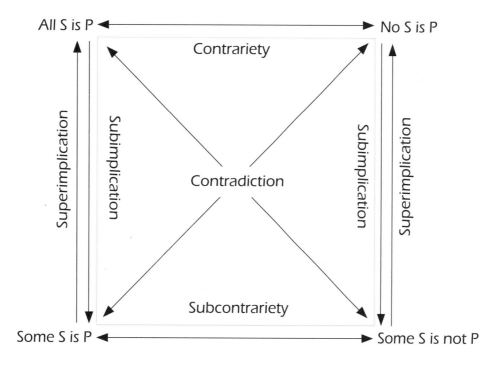

In the following problems, assume that the first statement in each set is true. Then determine the truth value of each remaining statement in the set. Circle *T* if it is true, *F* if it is false, and *?* if the truth value cannot be determined.

2. *All students are young people.*

    No students are young people.   T (F) ?

    Some students are young people.   (T) F ?

3. *No angels are demons.*

    Some angels are demons.   T (F) ?

    Some angels are not demons.   (T) F ?

4. *Some computers are word processors.*

    All computers are word processors.   T F (?)

    No computers are word processors.   T (F) ?

5. *Some laws are not biblical laws.*

    All laws are biblical laws.   T (F) ?

    No laws are biblical laws.   T F (?)

On the first line, translate the statement into standard categorical form. Do not abbreviate. On the second line, write the categorical statement which has the given relationship to the statement translated above it.

6. Students never eat frog legs.

   Standard form: No students are frog leg eaters.

   Contradiction: Some students are frog leg eaters.

7. Many children make mud pies.

   Standard form: Some children are mud pie makers.

   Subcontrariety: Some children are not mud pie makers.

8. Everybody here has eaten.

   Standard form: All people here are people who have eaten.

   Contrariety: No people here are people who have eaten.

9. A few of the meals were not appetizing.

   Standard form: Some meals were not appetizing meals.

   Superimplication: No meals were appetizing meals.

Challenge: Expand the "Relationships between Statements" chart in Lesson 9 (page 51) to include the relationships from the square of opposition.

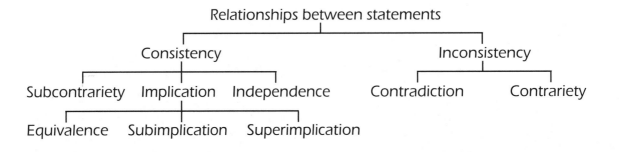

ANSWERS TO SELECTED UNIT 2 REVIEW EXERCISES

✒ ADDITIONAL EXERCISES FOR LESSON 6

1. The text says that statements are always either true or false. How would you respond to a scoffer who tried to deny this by claiming that there are no absolutely true statements?

   I would ask, "Is that true?" If he says yes, then he admits that there are true statements. If he says no, then he admits that there are true statements. In either case he contradicts himself.

2. If statements are always either true or false, how are we to understand statements for which we do not know the truth value? Consider this claim: "Somewhere in the infinite decimal expansion of the number pi ($\pi = 3.14159\ldots$) the digits 1234567890 appear in that order." No man knows if this is true or false. Is it a statement? Who does know the truth value?

   It is a statement. Truth does not depend upon what men know. Rather, truth is what God knows (Ps. 146:6; Jn. 14:6). God certainly knows the truth value of this statement.

3. There is a classic riddle of a missionary being threatened by natives in this way: "We will let you decide how you will die. If you say something true, you will be burned at the stake. If you say something false, you will be boiled in oil." The missionary escaped this dilemma by saying, "I will be boiled in oil." Was this sentence true, false, or nonsense? Explain.

   If the sentence were true, then he would be burned at the stake, making it false. If the sentence were false, then he would be boiled in oil, making it true. It appears impossible to nail down a truth value, so at least it appears to be more like nonsense than a statement.

4. When something is truly authoritative, you are required to respond to it submissively. The ultimate authority for Christians is the Bible. The Bible contains the types of sentences considered in this lesson. The submissive response to a command, such as Romans 12:1–2, is to obey it. What is a submissive response to a statement, such as Romans 5:8? What is a submissive response to questions, such as Romans 8:31–35? What type of sentence is Romans 11:33? What would be a submissive response to it?

   The submissive response to a statement is to believe it. The submissive response to a question is to answer it truthfully. Romans 11:33 is an exclamation. The submissive response to an exclamation is to say "Amen!" and mean it.

5. Consider Titus 1:12, in which Paul quotes a Cretan who said that Cretans are always liars. Should the Cretan's claim be considered nonsense? Why or why not?

That Cretan was probably not including himself in the set of Cretans who are liars—his universal claim about Cretans should not be taken as absolutely universal—so it should not be considered nonsense.

✒ ADDITIONAL EXERCISES FOR LESSON 7

1. Why do we usually consider self-reports to be true? Is there ever a situation in which we should challenge someone who makes a claim about his own desires, beliefs, or feelings? If so, give an example.

We assume in Christian charity that when someone speaks about their own thoughts, they are telling the truth. But in normal conversation, people often use the words of a self-report while actually making an objective statement, e.g. "I think 51 is a prime number." Rather than responding "Yes, it is true that you think that," a more natural response is "No, 51 is 3 x 17."

2. A tautology is true by logical structure and can take the form *p or not p.* Can you think of an example of a tautology in this form that someone might use in ordinary conversation?

Tautologies may appear in ordinary conversation when we are considering options, e.g., "You either believe the gospel, or you don't."

3. A self-contradiction is a statement which is false by logical structure. Is there ever an appropriate use of a self-contradiction?

One appropriate use is in proof by reductio ad absurdum, proving that a claim is false by showing that it leads to a self-contradiction. One example is seen in the answer to question 1 of the additional exercises for Lesson 6.

4. Consider Esther's statement in Esther 4:16, "If I perish, I perish." Is this a tautology?

Yes, following the Law of Identity.

5. What is the truth value of the statement *Unicorns have one horn?*

That depends on what the speaker means by the statement. If he means "Unicorns exist, and they have one horn," then it may be false. But more likely he means, "Within the realm of mythology, unicorns have one horn." Then we would consider it true by definition. Many difficulties arise in logic when making statements about subjects which do not exist, some of which we will consider later.

6. Which of the types of statements considered in this lesson should we understand this to be: "I think that triangles have three sides or I do not think that triangles have three sides"?

Though this includes characteristics of a tautology, self-report, and statements that are true by definition, overall it follows the pattern of a tautology, and should probably be considered such. If the statement used an "and" instead of an "or" it would be considered false, even though the person refers to his own thoughts.

✒ ADDITIONAL EXERCISES FOR LESSON 8

1. Consider the following supported statements. Explain how one would determine the truth value of each statement. Your options are *by authority, by experience,* or *by deductive reasoning.*
   a. Most teenage boys like to argue.

   Most likely true by experience.

   b. The capital city of Japan is Tokyo.

   Most likely true by authority (i.e. you believe someone who told you or some book you read).

   c. If you are reading this sentence then you can see.

   This is true by deduction (this book is not available in Braille).

   d. It's nine o'clock on a Saturday.

   The truth value is most likely known by experience (probably false).

   e. The product of two odd numbers is an odd number.

   Either true by deduction (it is fairly easy to prove this using basic algebra), or by authority (your teacher tells you, or you read it in a textbook).

f. It is easier for a camel to go through a needle's eye than for a rich man to enter into the kingdom of God.

True by authority.

2. Is it possible that all three methods (authority, experience, and deduction) may be used to determine the truth value of a given statement? Consider this claim: "In the absence of air, two different masses will fall toward the earth at the same rate." How might different people know that this is true?

A young student will first learn that this is true by authority. He may then verify it by experience. But it is also provable by deduction, as Galileo proves it in Dialogue of Two New Sciences.

3. Consider this claim: "Unicorns do not exist." Can the truth value of such a statement be determined by experience? If not, is there any way to determine the truth value of such statements?

Universal negative claims of this sort are not determined with certainty by experience; we cannot be in all places simultaneously to see that there are no unicorns there. The truth value of such statements can only be known with certainty by authority, by Someone who is in all places simultaneously.

4. Consider this claim: "California will probably experience a major earthquake within the next twenty years." Such a statement is supported by the inductive reasoning of experts. How does this method differ from the method of experience? of deductive reasoning? Can you think of other statements which are known to be true by inductive reasoning?

Inductive reasoning is a type of reasoning by experience in which the reasoner assumes that future experiences will be like past experiences, e.g. "In the past there have been major earthquakes in California every twenty years or so, especially under certain conditions," and so on. But experience is not always inductive reasoning; e.g., when I see that it is raining outside, I know it by experience, not by induction. Inductive reasoning differs from deductive by the certainty of the conclusion: deductive conclusions are either valid or invalid, while inductive conclusions are only probable, such as "The price of gasoline will be greater in ten years than it is now."

✒ ADDITIONAL EXERCISES FOR LESSON 9

1. The text says that when two statements can be true at the same time, they are consistent. Can two statements which happen to be false at the same time still be consistent? Consider these two false statements: "The apostle Paul spent his life in Germany" and "The apostle Peter was never married." Which relationships do these statements have with each other?

   Yes, two false statements can be consistent. The examples given are consistent; there is no logical conflict between them. They are also independent; their truth values do not affect each other. And if the text is correct, then all independent statements are consistent.

2. The text says that two statements are related by implication when the truth of the first requires the truth of the second. Can one false statement imply another false statement? For example, does "No dogs are mammals" imply that "Some dogs are not mammals"?

   Yes, one false statement can imply another, as in the given example. To check for implication, we ask ourselves "If the first statement were considered to be true, would the second necessarily be true?" And if no dogs were mammals, then any given set of dogs would not be mammals.

3. Can a false statement imply a true statement? For example, does "All mammals are dogs" imply that "Some mammals are dogs"?

   Yes, the statements given provide a good example showing that a false statement can imply a true statement. "All mammals are dogs" is false, but if it were true, then "Some mammals are dogs" would be true in consequence.

4. Is a statement equivalent to itself? If so, how else is a statement related to itself?

   A statement is of course equivalent to itself. This means that a statement is also related to itself by implication and consistency.

5. *No S is P* is equivalent to *No P is S*, and *Some S is P* is equivalent to *Some P is S* (when S and P are the same terms). Are statements of the form *All S is P* equivalent to *All P is S*? Are statements of the form *Some S is not P* equivalent to *Some P is not S*? If not, give examples of such pairs of statements that differ in truth value.

   All S is P is not equivalent to All P is S. For example, "All logic students are people" is true, "All people are logic students" is false. Similarly, Some S is not P is not equivalent to Some P is not S. "Some logic students are not people" is false, "Some people are not logic students" is true.

6. Can two statements with the same subject be logically independent?

   Yes. "George Washington was a Virginian" and "George Washington was a U.S. president" have the same subject, but are logically independent.

7. Give an example of consistent statements that are neither independent nor related by implication.

   Statements of the form Some S is P and Some S is not P are consistent, but not independent (if one is false, the other must be true) nor related by implication (one could be true and the other false). For example, "Some songs are poems" is consistent with "Some songs are not poems." But they cannot both be false, and the first does not imply the second.

8. Identify every relationship which exists between each of the following pairs of statements.

   This is a green apple.   Pluto is the ninth planet.

      Independence, consistency

   All roads lead to Rome.   Route 66 leads to Rome.

      Implication, consistency

   Some people like chocolate.   Everybody likes chocolate.

      Consistency

   No captains are cowards.   No cowards are captains.

      Equivalence, implication, consistency

   This is question 7.   This is question 8.

      Inconsistency

   Some frogs are princes.   Some princes are frogs.

      Equivalence, implication, consistency

The Bible is God's Word.   The Koran is not God's Word.

Consistency, independence

✒ ADDITIONAL EXERCISES FOR LESSON 10

1. Consider two people having an apparent disagreement (a difference in opinion). How could such a dispute change into a real disagreement?

   If they began to hold that what they were claiming was objectively true, not just their subjective opinion.

2. Why is it so important to define terms at the beginning of a debate?

   To avoid unnecessary verbal disagreements. If we must dispute, we should dispute not just about words (2 Tim. 2:14), but about ideas (2 Tim. 4:2).

3. Romans 4 seems to disagree with James 2:14–26 regarding faith and works in the justification of Abraham. Given that the infallible Scripture cannot contradict itself, what sort of disagreement might this be? Consider doing some further study on this issue.

   This is apparently a verbal disagreement. Paul and James have somewhat different meanings of the words "faith" and "justification" in mind, because they are dealing with different situations, different contexts. Several books discuss this issue. One is The Sufficiency of Scripture by Noel Weeks (published by Banner of Truth), especially the chapter titled "Words and Meaning Again."

✒ ADDITIONAL EXERCISES FOR LESSON 11

Translate the following statements so that they only use the verb of being.

1. The *Eagle* [the Apollo 11 spacecraft] has landed.

   The *Eagle* is a landed craft.

2. A prudent man conceals knowledge.

   A prudent man is a knowledge concealer.

3. Gentlemen in England now abed shall think themselves accursed they were not here.

   Gentlemen in England now abed shall be men who think themselves accursed they were not here.

4. Seventy-six trombones led the big parade.

   Seventy-six trombones were big-parade leaders.

5. The forests will echo with laughter.

   The forests will be echoing-with-laughter places.

6. We who have believed do enter that rest.

   We who have believed are rest enterers.

7. Angels we have heard on high.

   We have been angels-on-high hearers.

8. The great fish moved silently through the night water.

   The great fish was a silent-through-the-night-water mover.

✒ ADDITIONAL EXERCISES FOR LESSON 12

Translate the following statements into standard categorical form, and identify the quantity and quality of each.

1. In all labor there is a profit.

   All labor is profitable activity. – Universal affirmative

2. Most of the Trojans fell before Diomed's onslaught.

   Some Trojans were Diomed's victims. – Particular affirmative

3. The natural man does not receive the things of the Spirit of God.

   No natural man is a things-of-the-Spirit-of-God receiver. – Universal negative

4. Many brave souls went hurrying down to Hades.

   Some brave souls were down-to-Hades hurriers. – Particular affirmative

5. There is none righteous.

   No person is a righteous person. – Universal negative

6. A few names in Sardis have not defiled their garments.

   Some people in Sardis are not garment defilers. – Particular negative

7. The Argives held their peace as Hector spoke.

   All Argives present as Hector spoke were holders of their peace. – Universal af-firmative.

8. None of the Greeks approaching Troy spoke a word.

   No Troy-approaching Greeks were word speakers. – Universal negative

ADDITIONAL EXERCISES FOR LESSON 13

1. Fill in the blanks of the following chart.

No S is P	Universal negative	E
Some S is P	Particular affirmative	I
Some S is not P	Particular negative	O
All S is P	Universal affirmative	A
Some S is P	Particular affirmative	I
No S is P	Universal negative	E
All S is P	Universal affirmative	A
Some S is not P	Particular negative	O

2. Why do you suppose the vowels A, E, I, and O are used to represent the four categorical statements? What type of statement could we represent by the letter U?

   It has been claimed that A and I come from the first two vowels of the Latin "Affirmo" while the E and O come from the Latin "Nego." The letter U may conveniently rep-resent a statement of unknown quantity or quality.

3. Select any two of the following terms: *cats, dogs, reptiles, mammals.* Put the two terms you have selected as the subject and predicate of the four categorical statements, and put them in the square of opposition. Which statements are true? Which are false? How many true statements and how many false statements appear in every square of opposition?

   For example: All dogs are reptiles   No dogs are reptiles
                              F   T
                    Some dogs are reptiles   Some dogs are not reptiles
                              F   T

                   F   T
Whichever terms are chosen, two will be true and two will be false.

✐ ADDITIONAL EXERCISES FOR LESSON 14

Write the contradiction of the given statements. Which is the true statement: the given one, or its contradiction?

1. All men are sinners.

    Some men are not sinners. – The contradiction is true; Jesus is a man but not a sinner.

2. No pleasures are lawful activities.

    Some pleasures are lawful activities. – The contradiction is true, such as taking pleasure in your vocation.

3. Some Christians are Jews.

    No Christians are Jews. – The given statement is true; the apostles, for example.

4. Some worshiped beings are not idols.

    All worshiped beings are idols. – The given statement is true, for God is a worshiped being who is not an idol.

✐ ADDITIONAL EXERCISES FOR LESSON 15

1. Give an example of contrary statements that are both false. Give an example of contrary statements, one being true and the other false.

    Both false: All plants are flowers; No plants are flowers.
    One true, one false: All roses are flowers; No roses are flowers.

2. If someone is making a claim that you want to deny, which type of statement should you choose so that at least one of you is correct: the contradiction, or the contrary?

    The contradiction.

3. Consider these two inconsistent statements: *Pluto is a planet. Pluto is not a planet.* Are these statements related by contradiction or contrariety? Explain.

These statements are contradictory. One must be true, and the other false. They cannot both be false.

4. Can contrary statements both be true? What if the subject does not exist? For example, could "All Martian scientists are people eaters" and "No Martian scientists are people eaters" both be considered true, since there are no Martian scientists?

Normally (at least as considered in this text), contrary statements cannot both be true. Some logicians would argue that if the subject does not exist, as in this case, contrary statements can both be considered true. This touches on the issue of The Existential Presupposition, which can be read about in a college-level logic text, such as Irving Copi's Introduction to Logic, published by Macmillan.

✒ ADDITIONAL EXERCISES FOR LESSON 16

1. Give an example of subcontrary statements that are both true. Then give an example of subcontrary statements, one being true and the other false.

Both true: Some flowers are roses; Some flowers are not roses.
One true, one false: Some roses are flowers; Some roses are not flowers.

2. Without looking back at the text, restate the argument given as to why two statements related by subcontrariety cannot both be false.

See lesson 16.

3. Could subcontrary statements be considered false if the subject does not exist, e.g. "Some Martian scientists are people eaters" and "Some Martian scientists are not people eaters"?

They could be considered false if the statements are understood this way: "There exists at least one Martian scientist who is/is not a people eater." But generally they are not both considered to be false. This again touches on the Existential Presupposition problem.

4. If a given universal statement is true, can you figure out the truth value of the remaining statements on the square of opposition using only contradiction, contrariety, and subcontrariety? Can you do the same for a given false particular statement?

Yes. If a universal statement is true, then its contrary and contradiction are false, and the statement below it is true. If a particular statement is false, then its subcontrary and contradiction are true, and the statement above it is false.

✐ ADDITIONAL EXERCISES FOR LESSON 17

I. Find all the examples of subimplication that appear in the text prior to lesson 17.

There are several in lesson 9 and exercise 9 .

2. Some logicians translate *All S is P* as "If a thing is S then it is P" and *Some S is P* as "There exists an S which is P." Translated this way, a universal statement does not claim that the subject exists, but a particular statement does claim that something exists. How would this affect the relationship of subimplication? How would it affect the rest of the square of opposition? Does *All Martian scientists are people eaters* imply that *Some Martian scientists are people eaters*?

With this understanding of these statements, subimplication is no longer valid. "If a thing is a Martian scientist then it is a people eater" does not imply "There exists a Martian scientist which is a people eater," unless you count existence in the imagination. Translating statements in this way removes every relationship from the square of opposition except contradiction. To maintain the relationships, one must assume that the subject of the statements in the square of opposition exists.

✐ ADDITIONAL EXERCISES FOR LESSON 18

I. Some logic texts consider subimplication and superimplication as two ways of looking at the same relationship, called *subalternation.* Thus, the square of opposition would only have one arrow on each side pointing both up and down. With this understanding, draw a genus and species chart which includes the following terms: *consistency, contradiction, contrariety, equivalence, implication, inconsistency, independence, relationship between statements, subalternation, subcontrariety, subimplication, superimplication.*

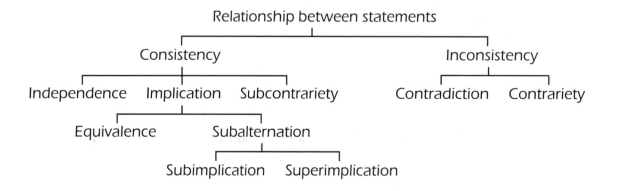

Identify the relationship which exists between the first and second statement given.

2. All czars are dukes. Some czars are dukes.   Subimplication
3. Some spiders are insects. No spiders are insects.   Contradiction
4. All meats are desserts. No meats are desserts.   Contrariety
5. Some peptides are not acids. No peptides are acids.   Superimplication
6. Some castles are not palaces. All castles are palaces.   Contradiction
7. Some spies are touts. Some spies are not touts.   Subcontrariety

Name the square of opposition relationship being described.

8. If a statement is true, the statement of a different quantity and quality is false.

   Contradiction

9. If a particular statement is false, the universal of the same quality must be false.

   Superimplication

10. Both statements of the same quantity can be true, but they cannot both be false.

    Subcontrariety

11. If a universal statement is true, the particular of the same quality must be true.

    Subimplication

12. Both statements of the same quantity can be false, but they cannot both be true.

    Contrariety

Assume the first statement in the set is false. Then determine the corresponding truth value of the remaining statements in the set. Your options are *true, false,* or *cannot be determined.*

13. Assume false: <u>All caps are derbies.</u>
    Determine truth value: *No caps are derbies; Some caps are derbies; Some caps are not derbies.*

    Cannot be determined; Cannot be determined; True

14. Assume false: <u>No newts are salamanders.</u>
    Determine: *Some newts are salamanders; Some newts are not salamanders; All newts are salamanders.*

    True; Cannot be determined; Cannot be determined

15. Assume false: <u>Some emus are ostriches.</u>
    Determine: *All emus are ostriches; No emus are ostriches; Some emus are not ostriches.*

    False; True; True

16. Assume false: <u>Some swamis are not punjabis.</u>
    Determine: *All swamis are punjabis; No swamis are punjabis; Some swamis are punjabis.*

    True; False; True

UNIT THREE

SYLLOGISMS AND VALIDITY

CONTENTS

✒ EXERCISE 18

Underline the conclusion in each of the following arguments.

1. All theology is a study in infinity, so <u>all calculus problems are theology</u>, because all calculus problems are a study in infinity.

2. All space stations are important research, but some space stations are not a product of American ingenuity. Therefore <u>some important research is not a product of American ingenuity</u>.

3. <u>Some pagans are idolaters</u>, because no pagans are Christians, and no Christians are idolaters.

4. All objects in free fall are weightless, and all meteoroids are objects in free fall. Therefore <u>all meteoroids are weightless</u>.

5. All marsupials are pouched animals, and some marsupials are not Australian mammals. Consequently, <u>some Australian mammals are not pouched animals</u>.

6. <u>Some Socratic sages are not perspicacious people</u>, since some Socratic sages are metaphorical masters, and some perspicacious people are also metaphorical masters.

7. All murderers are criminals, and some heroes of the faith are murderers, from which it follows that <u>some criminals are heroes of the faith</u>.

8. No street legal vehicles are stock cars. Thus <u>no racing car is street legal</u>, since all stock cars are racing cars.

9. <u>Some conclusions are not easily located statements</u>, for all easily located statements are sentences at the end of arguments, and some sentences at the end of arguments are not conclusions.

10. Given that some pagan literature is great writing, and no great writing is worthless instructional material, we must conclude that <u>some pagan literature is not worthless instructional material</u>.

✒ *EXERCISE 19*

Identify the major, minor and middle terms for each syllogism. The syllogisms are not necessarily in standard order.

1. All theology is a study in infinity, so all calculus problems are theology, because all calculus problems are a study in infinity.

    Major term: Theology

    Minor term: Calculus problems

    Middle term: Study in infinity

2. All space stations are important research, but some space stations are not a product of American ingenuity. Therefore some important research is not a product of American ingenuity.

    Major term: Product of American ingenuity

    Minor term: Important research

    Middle term: Space stations

3. Some pagans are idolaters, because no pagans are Christians, and no Christians are idolaters.

    Major term: Idolaters

    Minor term: Pagans

    Middle term: Christians

4. All objects in free fall are weightless, and all meteoroids are objects in free fall. Therefore all meteoroids are weightless.

    Major term: Weightless (objects)

    Minor term: Meteoroids

    Middle term: Objects in free fall

5. All marsupials are pouched animals, and some marsupials are not Australian mammals. Consequently, some Australian mammals are not pouched animals.

    Major term: Pouched animals

    Minor term: Australian mammals

    Middle term: Marsupials

Rewrite the following arguments into standard order for categorical syllogisms.

6. Some Socratic sages are not perspicacious people, since some Socratic sages are metaphorical masters, and some perspicacious people are also metaphorical masters.

    Some perspicacious people are metaphorical masters.
    Some Socratic sages are metaphorical masters.
    Therefore, some Socratic sages are not perspicacious people.

7. All murderers are criminals, and some heroes of the faith were murderers, from which it follows that some criminals are heroes of the faith.

    Some heroes of the faith were murderers.
    All murderers are criminals.
    Therefore, some criminals are heroes of the faith.

8. No street legal vehicles are stock cars. Thus no racing car is street legal, since all stock cars are racing cars.

    No street legal vehicles are stock cars.
    All stock cars are racing cars.
    Therefore, no racing car is a street legal vehicle.

9. Some conclusions are not easily located statements, for all easily located statements are sentences at the end of arguments, and some sentences at the end of arguments are not conclusions.

    All easily located statements are sentences at the end of arguments.
    Some sentences at the end of arguments are not conclusions.
    Therefore, some conclusions are not easily located statements.

10. Given that some pagan literature is great writing, and no great writing is worthless instructional material, we must conclude that some pagan literature is not worthless instructional material.

    No great writing is worthless instructional material.
    Some pagan literature is great writing.
    Therefore, some pagan literature is not worthless instructional material.

✒ *EXERCISE 20*

Write the form (mood and figure) of the following syllogisms on the blank to the right. The syllogisms are in standard order.

1. All Bibles are books.

   Some periodicals are not books.

   Therefore some periodicals are not Bibles.   AOO-2

2. Some speeches are sermons.

   No sermons are short events.

   Thus some short events are not speeches.   IEO-4

3. All students are geniuses.

   Some blondes are students.

   Consequently, some blondes are geniuses.   AII-1

4. No fish are mammals.

   No fish are snakes.

   So no snakes are mammals.   EEE-3

Rewrite these syllogisms in standard order and give their mood and figure.

5. All combatants are fighters, so all Spartans are fighters, since all Spartans are combatants.

   All combatants are fighters.
   All Spartans are combatants.
   Therefore, all Spartans are fighters.

   Mood and figure: AAA-1

6. Some sailors are not poets, because all sailors are mariners, but some poets are not mariners.

   Some poets are not mariners.
   All sailors are mariners.
   Therefore, some sailors are not poets.

   Mood and figure: OAO-2

7. All books are paper, and some plaques are not paper. Hence, some books are not plaques.

Some plaques are not paper.
All books are paper.
Therefore, some books are not plaques.

Mood and figure: OAO-2   (Note this is the same as the previous problem)

✒ EXERCISE 21

Write out the schemas for the given forms.

I. EIO-I

> No M is P
> Some S is M
> ∴ Some S is not P

2. IAI-2

> Some P is M
> All S is M
> ∴ Some S is P

3. AOO-3

> All M is P
> Some M is not S
> ∴ Some S is not P

4. OIO-4

> Some P is not M
> Some M is S
> ∴ Some S is not P

Now develop your own syllogisms to meet the requirements of the given form. Make sure your syllogisms are in standard order.

5. AEE-I

> All women are people.
> No men are women.
> Therefore, no men are people.

6. EAO-2

> No men are women.
> All mothers are women.
> Therefore, some mothers are not men.

7. AII-3

> All men are people.
> Some men are fathers.
> Therefore, some fathers are people.

8. EAE-4

> No men are women.
> All women are people.
> Therefore, no people are men.

✒ EXERCISE 22

Test the following syllogisms by counterexample. If no counterexample is possible, write "valid."

1. Some cherubim are not angels.
   Some angels are not seraphim.
   Therefore, all seraphim are cherubim.

   Some cherries are not apples.
   Some apples are not strawberries.
   Therefore, all strawberries are cherries.

2. No wind instruments are guitars.
   All wind instruments are expensive instruments.
   Therefore, no expensive instrument is a guitar.

   No watermelons are grapes.
   All watermelons are edible things.
   Therefore, no edible things are grapes.

3. All NIV Bibles are Zondervan publications.
   Some KJV Bibles are not Zondervan publications.
   Therefore, no KJV Bible is an NIV Bible.

   All snakes are reptiles.
   Some animals are not reptiles.
   Therefore, no animals are snakes.

4. Some Baptists are not Presbyterians.
    No Nazarene is a Baptist.
    Therefore, all Nazarenes are Presbyterians.

    Some bones are not plastic things.
    No nectarines are bones.
    Therefore, all nectarines are plastic things.

5. All Calvinists are predestinarians.
    No predestinarian is an Arminian.
    Therefore, some Arminians are not Calvinists.

    Valid

6. Some colds are not fatal diseases.
    All cancers are fatal diseases.
    Therefore, some cancers are not colds.

    Some creatures are not felines.
    All cats are felines.
    Therefore, some cats are not creatures.

Challenge: Work through the 256 forms of syllogisms in Appendix B, using counterexamples to determine validity. There are 232 invalid forms and 24 valid ones. As you work through them, remember that if you cannot figure out a counterexample, it is either valid or you need to be more creative. Also, you would be greatly assisted in working through them more quickly if you recall what you learned about the relationships between statements. Good luck!

AAA-1	EAE-1, EAE-2
AAI-1, AAI-3, AAI-4	EAO-1, EAO-2, EAO-3, EAO-4
AEE-2, AEE-4	EIO-1, EIO-2, EIO-3, EIO-4
AEO-2, AEO-4	IAI-3, IAI-4
AII-1, AII-3	OAO-3
AOO-2	

✒ *EXERCISE 23*

1. What is a *distributed* term?

> A distributed term is a term that refers to all members of its category.

Underline the distributed terms in the following statements.

2. Some athletes are not <u>honors students</u>.

3. No <u>clear liquid</u> is a <u>solid object</u>.

4. Some politicians are corrupt men.

5. All <u>chefs</u> are contented people.

6. No <u>Bible reader</u> is an <u>ignorant person</u>.

7. Some millionaires are not <u>lazy men</u>.

8. Some Baptists are immersionists.

Underline the distributed terms in the following syllogisms.

9. No <u>wind instruments</u> are <u>guitars</u>.

   All <u>wind instruments</u> are expensive instruments.

   Therefore, no <u>expensive instrument</u> is a <u>guitar</u>.

10. Some colds are not <u>fatal diseases</u>.

   All <u>cancers</u> are fatal diseases.

   Therefore, some cancers are not <u>colds</u>.

✒ EXERCISE 24

In the following exercise, analyze the syllogisms. Identify which rules are violated in the syllogism by writing the name of the fallacy or fallacies. If no fallacy is made, write "valid." The premises are *not* necessarily in standard order. (Hint: the first syllogism violates three rules).

1. Some chefs are not fat people.
    No fat person is a contented person.
    Therefore, all chefs are contented people.

    Illicit minor, Two negative premises, Negative premise & affirmative conclusion

2. All water is clear liquid.
    No clear liquid is a solid object.
    Therefore, some water is not a solid object.

    Valid

3. Some Christians are not Bible-readers.
    No Bible-reader is an ignorant person.
    Therefore, no ignorant person is a Christian.

    Two negative premises, Illicit major

4. All Muslims are Hindus.
    All Hindus are Christians.
    Therefore, some Christians are not Muslims.

    Two affirmative premises & negative conclusion

5. No dog is a cat.
    Some cats are female.
    Therefore, some dogs are female.

    Negative premise & affirmative conclusion

6. Some politicians are corrupt men.
   Some corrupt men are Mafia members.
   Therefore, some politicians are Mafia members.

   Undistributed middle

7. No honors students are rugby players.
   Some athletes are rugby players.
   Therefore, some athletes are not honors students.

   Valid

8. Some challenging games are not fun games.
   Some fun games are not chess.
   Therefore, all challenging games are chess.

   Two negative premises, Illicit minor, Negative premise & affirmative conclusion

9. Some professionals are millionaires.
   Some millionaires are not lazy men.
   Therefore, no lazy men are professionals.

   Undistributed middle, Illicit major

10. Some Baptists are immersionists.
    No Presbyterian is a Baptist.
    Therefore, some Presbyterians are not immersionists.

    Illicit major

Challenge: For more practice, find the fallacies made by syllogisms used in previous exercises.

Exercise 18
1. Und. middle
2. Ill. minor
3. 2 neg. prem., Neg. prem. + aff. concl.
5. Ill. major
6. Ill. major, Und. middle, 2 aff. prem. + neg. concl.
8. Ill. minor
9. Und. middle

Exercise 20
2. Ill. major
4. 2 neg. prem.
6. Ill. major
7. Ill. major

Exercise 21
2. Und. middle
3. Ill. major
4. Ill. major
5. Ill. major
8. Ill. minor

Exercise 22
1. 2 neg. prem., Neg. prem. + aff. concl.
2. Ill. minor
3. Ill. minor
4. 2 neg. prem., Neg. prem. + aff. concl.
6. Ill. major

Exercise 23
9. Ill. minor
10. Ill. major

✒ *EXERCISE 25*

Write schemas of syllogisms which have the given fallacies.

1. Illicit major, illicit minor.

> Some P is M
> Some S is not M
> ∴ No S is P

2. Two negative premises, undistributed middle.

> Some M is not P
> Some M is not S
> ∴ No S is P

3. Two negative premises, negative premise and affirmative conclusion.

> No P is M
> No M is S
> ∴ All S is P

4. Two affirmative premises and a negative conclusion, illicit major.

> All M is P
> All S is M
> ∴ Some S is not P

5. Illicit major, illicit minor, undistributed middle, and two affirmative premises and a negative conclusion.

Some M is P
Some S is M
∴ No S is P

ANSWERS TO SELECTED UNIT 3 REVIEW EXERCISES

✒ ADDITIONAL EXERCISES FOR LESSON 19

I. Locate the conclusion in each of the sample arguments.

1. No true socialist is a millionaire, but some Russians are millionaires. Therefore, <u>some Russians are not true socialists.</u>
2. All modern high-resolution images are digital pictures, so <u>some photographs from satellites are modern high-resolution images</u>, since some digital pictures are photographs from satellites.
3. <u>Some robots are not programmed humanoids</u>, because some robots are androids, and all androids are programmed humanoids.
4. All epic poems are works of great artistry. Hence, given that no nursery rhymes are works of great artistry, <u>no nursery rhymes are epic poems.</u>
5. No tele-judges are supreme court justices, and some tele-judges are not public defenders. Thus, <u>some supreme court justices are not public defenders.</u>
6. No high-school mathematics is advanced particle physics. Consequently, <u>some advanced algebra must be advanced particle physics</u>, for all advanced algebra is high-school mathematics.
7. <u>Some secret agents are not arrogant mothers</u>, because some arrogant mothers are mid-management secretaries, but no mid-management secretaries are secret agents.
8. Some chanting story-tellers are rap singers, so <u>some bards are rap singers</u>, since all chanting story-tellers are bards.
9. All football games are sporting events, and all football games are physically exhausting activities. Clearly, <u>all sporting events are physically exhausting activities</u>.
10. Some professional nurses are not licensed medical practitioners. Therefore <u>all graduates of medical school are licensed medical practitioners</u>, for some graduates of medical school are professional nurses.

2. How many of the sample arguments have conclusions as the final sentence?

The conclusion is the final sentence in four of the ten sample arguments.

✒ ADDITIONAL EXERCISES FOR LESSON 20

I. Locate the major term, minor term, and middle term for each of the sample arguments.

	Major term	Minor term	Middle term
1.	True socialists	Russians	Millionaires
2.	Modern, high resolution images	Photographs from satellites	Digital pictures

3. Programmed humanoids	Robots	Androids
4. Epic poems	Nursery rhymes	Works of great artistry
5. Public defenders	Supreme court justices	Tele-judges
6. Advanced particle physics	Advanced algebra	High school math
7. Arrogant mothers	Secret agents	Mid-management secretaries
8. Rap singers	Bards	Chanting story-tellers
9. Physically exhausting activities	Sporting events	Football games
10. Licensed medical practitioners	Graduates of medical school	Professional nurses

2. Arrange the sample arguments into standard form syllogisms.

1. No true socialist is a millionaire.
   Some Russians are millionaires.
   ∴ Some Russians are not true socialists.

2. All modern high-resolution images are digital pictures.
   Some digital pictures are photographs from satellites.
   ∴ Some photographs from satellites are modern high-resolution images.

3. All androids are programmed humanoids.
   Some robots are androids.
   ∴ Some robots are not programmed humanoids.

4. All epic poems are works of great artistry.
   No nursery rhymes are works of great artistry.
   ∴ No nursery rhymes are epic poems.

5. Some tele-judges are not public defenders.
   No tele-judges are supreme court justices.
   ∴ Some supreme court justices are not public defenders.

6. No high-school mathematics is advanced particle physics.
   All advanced algebra is high-school mathematics.
   ∴ Some advanced algebra is advanced particle physics.

7. Some arrogant mothers are mid-management secretaries.
   No mid-management secretaries are secret agents.
   ∴ Some secret agents are not arrogant mothers.

8. Some chanting story-tellers are rap singers.
   All chanting story-tellers are bards.
   ∴ Some bards are rap singers.

9. All football games are physically exhausting activities.
   All football games are sporting events.
   ∴ All sporting events are physically exhausting activities.

10. Some professional nurses are not licensed medical practitioners.
Some graduates of medical school are professional nurses.
∴ All graduates of medical school are licensed medical practitioners.

✒ ADDITIONAL EXERCISES FOR LESSON 21 AND LESSON 22

I. Write out the schemas for the sample arguments.

1. No P is M.
   Some S are M.
   ∴ Some S are not P.
2. All P are M.
   Some M are S.
   ∴ Some S are P.
3. All M are P.
   Some S are M.
   ∴ Some S are not P.
4. All P are M.
   No S are M.
   ∴ No S are P.
5. Some M are not P.
   No M are S.
   ∴ Some S are not P.

6. No M is P.
   All S is M.
   ∴ Some S is P.
7. Some P are M.
   No M are S.
   ∴ Some S are not P.
8. Some M are P.
   All M are S.
   ∴ Some S are P.
9. All M are P.
   All M are S.
   ∴ All S are P.
10. Some M are not P.
    Some S are M.
    ∴ All S are P.

2. Determine their mood and figure.

1. EIO-2
2. AII-4
3. AIO-1
4. AEE-2
5. OEO-3

6. EAI-1
7. IEO-4
8. IAI-3
9. AAA-3
10. OIA-1

3. Write the schemas for each of the following moods and figures, and use the schemas to then write your own standard-form syllogisms: AII-1, IEO-2, EAO-3, OAO-4.

AII-1	All M is P	All mice are rodents.
	Some S is M	Some pests are mice.
	∴ Some S is P	∴ Some pests are rodents.

IEO-2	Some P is M	Some elves are swift travelers.
	No S is M	No dwarves are swift travelers.
	∴ Some S is not P	∴ Some dwarves are not elves.

EAO-3   No M is P   No Geats are Danes.
         All M is S   All Geats are Swedes.
         ∴ Some S is not P   ∴ Some Swedes are not Danes.

OAO-4   Some P is not M   Some propitiations are not burnt offerings.
         All M is S   All burnt offerings are sacrifices.
         ∴ Some S is not P   ∴ Some sacrifices are not propitiations.

✒ ADDITIONAL EXERCISES FOR LESSON 23

1. Which of the sample arguments appear to be valid?

> Numbers 1, 4, and 8 are valid.

2. Of those, which appear to be sound? Why?

> # 1 appears to be sound. Can a *true* socialist be a millionaire?
> # 4 appears to be sound. Are any nursery rhymes works of great artistry?
> # 8 does not appear to be sound. Not all chanting story tellers are bards.

✒ ADDITIONAL EXERCISE FOR LESSON 24

Three of the sample arguments are valid. Identify them and write counter-examples for the seven invalid sample arguments.

1. Valid
2. All oats are grains.
   Some grains are rice.
   ∴ Some rice is oats.
3. All gorillas are mammals.
   Some apes are gorillas.
   ∴ Some apes are not mammals.
4. Valid
5. Some harps are not pianos.
   No harps are grand pianos.
   ∴ Some grand pianos are not pianos.
6. No mammals are reptiles.
   All apes are mammals.
   ∴ Some apes are reptiles.
7. Some fruits are bananas.
   No bananas are apples.
   ∴ Some apples are not fruit.

8. Valid
9. All Huguenots are Protestants.
   All Huguenots are French people.
   ∴ All French people are Protestants.
10. Some wheeled vehicles are not motorcycles.
    Some airplanes are wheeled vehicles.
    ∴ All airplanes are motorcycles.

ADDITIONAL EXERCISES FOR LESSONS 25 AND 26

I. Identify the distributed terms in the sample arguments.

The distributed terms are underlined:
1. No <u>true socialist</u> is <u>a millionaire</u>.
   Some Russians are millionaires.
   ∴ Some Russians are not <u>true socialists</u>.
2. All <u>modern high-resolution images</u> are digital pictures.
   Some digital pictures are photographs from satellites.
   ∴ Some photographs from satellites are modern high-resolution images.
3. All <u>androids</u> are programmed humanoids.
   Some robots are androids.
   ∴ Some robots are not <u>programmed humanoids</u>.
4. All <u>epic poems</u> are works of great artistry.
   No <u>nursery rhymes</u> are <u>works of great artistry</u>.
   ∴ No <u>nursery rhymes</u> are <u>epic poems</u>.
5. Some tele-judges are not <u>public defenders</u>.
   No <u>tele-judges</u> are <u>supreme court justices</u>.
   ∴ Some supreme court justices are not <u>public defenders</u>.
6. No <u>high-school mathematics</u> is <u>advanced particle physics</u>.
   All <u>advanced algebra</u> is high-school mathematics.
   ∴ Some advanced algebra is advanced particle physics.
7. Some arrogant mothers are mid-management secretaries.
   No <u>mid-management secretaries</u> are <u>secret agents</u>.
   ∴ Some secret agents are not <u>arrogant mothers</u>.
8. Some chanting story-tellers are rap singers.
   All <u>chanting story-tellers</u> are bards.
   ∴ Some bards are rap singers.
9. All <u>football games</u> are physically exhausting activities.
   All <u>football games</u> are sporting events.
   ∴ All <u>sporting events</u> are physically exhausting activities.
10. Some professional nurses are not <u>licensed medical practitioners</u>.
    Some graduates of medical school are professional nurses.
    ∴ All <u>graduates of medical school</u> are licensed medical practitioners.

2. Determine the formal fallacies made in each of the sample arguments.

1. None
2. Und. middle
3. 2 aff. prem + neg. concl., Ill. major
4. None
5. 2 neg. prem.
6. Neg. prem. + aff. concl.
7. Ill. major
8. None
9. Ill. minor
10. Neg. prem. + aff. concl., Und. middle, Ill. minor

UNIT 4 FOUR

ARGUMENTS IN NORMAL ENGLISH

CONTENTS

✒ EXERCISE 26

Write two valid immediate inferences for each of the statements given. Identify the immediate inferences as either *converse, obverse,* or *contrapositive.*

1. All things that glitter are gold.

> No things that glitter are non-gold. – Obverse
> All non-gold is a non-glittering thing. – Contrapositive

2. No emperors were philosophers.

> All emperors were non-philosophers. – Obverse
> No philosophers were emperors. – Converse

3. Some prophets are pagans.

> Some prophets are not non-pagans. – Obverse
> Some pagans are prophets. – Converse

4. Some mathematicians are not teachers.

> Some mathematicians are non-teachers. – Obverse
> Some non-teachers are not non-mathematicians. – Contrapositive

Write statements with the given criteria, which will show that the immediate inference given is not valid for the given type of statement.

5. A false A statement which has a true converse.

> All women are mothers.

6. A true O statement which has a false converse.

Some mammals are not dogs.

7. A false I statement which has a true contrapositive.

Some dogs are cats.

✒ EXERCISE 27

Translate the following arguments into standard-form categorical syllogisms. Note that they may not be in proper order. Also, find and identify the one invalid syllogism.

1. Some Christians are Calvinists, but no Christians are unbelievers. Therefore some Calvinists are believers.

   All Christians are believers.
   Some Christians are Calvinists.
   Therefore, some Calvinists are believers.

2. All mumbling is murmuring, so all mumbling is nonsensical, since no murmuring is sensical.

   No murmuring is sense.
   All mumbling is murmuring.
   Therefore, no mumbling is sense.

3. All perfect beings are nonhuman, since all mortals are imperfect, and no humans are immortals.

   All humans are mortals.
   No mortals are perfect beings.
   Therefore, no perfect beings are humans.

4. All eighth graders are less than six feet tall, because all poor logicians are non-eighth graders, and nobody six feet tall or more is a good logician.

   All six-footers are poor logicians.
   No poor logicians are eighth-graders.
   Therefore, no eighth-graders are six-footers.

5. Some non-adults are not immature people, but no mature people are impatient people. We must conclude that some adults are patient people.

    All mature people are patient people.
    Some mature people are not adults.
    Therefore, some adults are patient people.   INVALID

6. No things that glitter are non-gold, and all gold is expensive. Thus, nothing that glitters is inexpensive.

    All gold things are expensive things.
    All things that glitter are gold things.
    Therefore, all things that glitter are expensive things.

✒ *EXERCISE 28*

Translate the following statements in normal English into standard categorical form.

1. God is good.

    All God is a good being.

2. As many as are led by the Spirit of God, these are sons of God.

    All people led by the Spirit of God are sons of God.

3. If you sin then you are a lawbreaker.

    All sinners are lawbreakers.

4. Not everybody will come.

    Some people are not people who will come.

5. A soft answer turns away wrath.

    All soft answers are wrath deflectors.

6. If anyone loves the world, the love of the Father is not in him.

    No lovers of the world are people with the love of the Father.

7. Many antichrists have come.

    Some antichrists have been comers.

8. I believe.

    All I am a believer.

9. The Pharisees sit in Moses' seat.

    All the Pharisees are in Moses' seat sitters.

10. The love of most will grow cold.

Some love will be cold love.

✒ EXERCISE 29

Translate the following statements in normal English into standard categorical form.

1. Wherever you go, there you are.

   All places you go are places you are.

2. You may prepare it however you like.

   All ways you like to prepare it are ways you may prepare it.

3. Unless you repent, you too will perish.

   All non-repenters will be perishers.

4. He never did anything wrong.

   No times are times he did wrong.

5. You will reap what you sow.

   All things you sow are things you will reap.

6. He gets sick whenever he drinks milk.

   All times he drinks milk are times he gets sick.

7. Righteousness is found only in the Lord.

   All righteousness is a thing found in the Lord.

8. God does whatever He pleases.

   All things He pleases are things God does.

9. You always hurt the one you love.

   All people you love are people you hurt.

10. Nobody leaves except those who have finished.

All leavers are finishers.

✒ *EXERCISE 30*

Translate the following arguments into standard categorical form.

1. Happy is the land that has no history, and King Frank's land has no history. We must conclude that King Frank's land is happy.

> All lands without history are happy lands.
> All King Frank's land is a land without history.
> Therefore, all King Frank's land is a happy land.

2. None but the wise are truly happy, so Solomon was happy, since he was so wise.

> All truly happy people are wise people.
> All Solomon was a wise person.
> Therefore, all Solomon was a truly happy person.

3. Some people are not Christ's disciples, for whoever turns away cannot be His disciple, and many people turn away.

> No people who turn away are Christ's disciples.
> Some people are people who turn away.
> Therefore, some people are not Christ's disciples.

4. All sciences except logic study the tangible, and chemistry is not logic. Thus, chemistry is a study of the tangible.

> All non-logic sciences are tangible studies.
> All chemistry is a non-logic science.
> Therefore, all chemistry is a tangible study.

5. Write a counterexample to the one invalid argument in this exercise.

Number 2 is invalid. Here is a counterexample:

All women are people.
All Solomon was a person.
Therefore, all Solomon was a woman.

✒ EXERCISE 31

Translate the following enthymemes into standard-form syllogisms. Assume the enthymeme is valid, and place parentheses around the assumed statement. Number 5 assumes the conclusion.

1. Tomorrow is not Tuesday, therefore tomorrow we will not have a test.

> (All test days are Tuesdays.)
> No tomorrow is a Tuesday.
> Therefore, no tomorrow is a test day.

2. No enthymemes are complete, so some arguments are incomplete.

> No enthymemes are complete arguments.
> (Some arguments are enthymemes.)
> Therefore, some arguments are not complete arguments.

3. Some young people are not rebels, since not everyone rebels as a teenager.

> Some teenagers are not rebels.
> (All teenagers are young people.)
> Therefore, some young people are not rebels.

4. Most Russians are not capitalists, because communists are not capitalists.

> No communists are capitalists.
> (Some Russians are communists.)
> Therefore, some Russians are not capitalists.

5. God does whatever He pleases, and He is pleased to save sinners. So . . . .

All things He pleases are things God does.
All saving of sinners is a thing He pleases.
(Therefore, all saving of sinners is a thing God does.)

✒ EXERCISE 32

Repeat the above exercise using these enthymemes, all taken from Scripture.

1. "This man is not from God, for he does not keep the Sabbath" (John 9:16).

    (All men from God are Sabbath keepers.)
    No this man is a Sabbath keeper.
    Therefore, no this man is a man from God.

2. "I will fear no evil, for you are with me" (Psalm 23:4).

    (No person with you will be an evil fearer.)
    All I am a person with you.
    Therefore, no I will be an evil fearer.

3. "You are worthy, our Lord and God, to receive glory . . . for you created all things" (Rev. 4:11).

    (All creators of all things are beings worthy of glory.)
    All God is the creator of all things.
    Therefore, all God is a being worthy of glory.

4. "The promise comes by faith, so that it may be by grace" (Rom. 4:16).

    (All things that come by faith are things by grace.)
    All the promise is a thing that comes by faith.
    Therefore, all the promise is a thing by grace.

5. "Here are my mother and my brothers! For whoever does the will of my Father in heaven is my brother and sister and mother" (Matt. 12:49-50).

All people who do the Father's will are my family members.
(All the people here are people who do the Father's will.)
Therefore, all the people here are my family members.

✒ EXERCISE 33

Analyze each of the following arguments and write down its form in the blank provided: *pure hypothetical, modus ponens, modus tollens, affirming the consequent,* or *denying the antecedent.*

1. If you are lazy, then you will be poor. Henry is poor, and it follows that he is therefore lazy.

   Affirming the consequent

2. The Bible teaches that if a man is generous, then he will prosper. We know that Mike is not generous, and therefore he cannot prosper.

   Denying the antecedent

3. If you speak too much, sin will not be absent. If sin is not absent, then it is present. Thus if you speak too much, sin is present.

   Pure hypothetical

4. If a ministry is of God, then it will succeed. The Mormon church is successful. We can conclude that it is blessed by God.

   Affirming the consequent

5. If you are kind to the poor, then you are lending to the Lord. Paul is kind to the poor. He is therefore lending to the Lord.

   Modus ponens

6. If you visit your neighbor too much he will get sick of you. My neighbor is not sick of me, so I don't think I visit too much.

   Modus tollens

7. If you don't answer a fool according to his folly, then he will think that he is wise. Sharon did not answer him that way. He must think he is wise.

   Modus ponens

8. If a country is rebellious, it has many rulers. Argentina has had many rulers; it must be a rebellious country.

    Affirming the consequent

9. If a man is lawless, even his prayers are detestable. Larry is not at all a lawless man. So his prayers must not be detestable.

    Denying the antecedent

10. "If you are willing, you can make me clean." "I am willing," Jesus said. "Be clean."

    Modus ponens

11. If recycling were necessary, then it would be profitable. Recycling is not yet profitable. So it must not be necessary.

    Modus tollens

12. If a man gives gifts, then everyone wants to be his friend. Everyone wants to be Gordon's friend. Gordon must give out a lot of gifts.

    Affirming the consequent

13. If they receive you, they receive me. If they receive me, then they receive Him who sent me. So if they receive you, they receive Him who sent me.

    Pure hypothetical

14. If I kill you, then you will die. I promise that I will never kill you. Therefore, you will never die!

    Denying the antecedent

15. If you flog a mocker, then the simple will learn prudence. We don't flog mockers. That must be why we have so many imprudent people.

    Denying the antecedent

16. If you are rich, then many will want to be your friend. No one wants to be Jessica's friend. She must not be rich.

    Modus tollens

17. If you honor the Lord with your wealth, then He will bless you greatly. Mr. Spence has always honored the Lord this way. He will be blessed.

    Modus ponens

18. If you fear the Lord, then you will love wisdom. A man who hates wisdom must not fear the Lord.

    Modus tollens

19. If you are a Christian, then you will read your Bible. I know a man who reads the Bible. He must be a Christian.

    Affirming the consequent

20. If they had belonged to us, they would have remained with us. But they went out from us. This showed that they did not belong to us.

    Modus tollens

✒ EXERCISE 34

Analyze the following paragraph. Separate the various arguments (there are four), and determine whether they are valid or not. Identify each argument by name.

If Paul went to Ephesus, then he wouldn't write the Ephesians a letter. But he did write them a letter, which means that he didn't go to Ephesus. But if Paul didn't go to Ephesus, then he would not have known the people there. We know, however, that Paul did go to Ephesus, therefore he did know the people there. If he knew the people in Ephesus, then he would have known the saints in Colossae too. But we know that he did not know the Christians in Colossae, which means that he didn't know the Ephesians. If Paul didn't know the Ephesians, then he would have written them a letter. He wrote them a letter, and this proves that he did not know them.

1. E ⊃ L   E = Paul went to Ephesus.
    ~L   L = Paul did not write the Ephesians a letter.
    ∴ ~E

    Name: Modus tollens   Valid: Yes

2. G ⊃ K   G = Paul did not go to Ephesus.
    ~G   K = Paul did not know the people there.
    ∴ ~K

    Name: Denying the antecedent   Valid: No

3. E ⊃ C   E = Paul knew the Ephesians.
    ~C   C = Paul knew the Colossians.
    ∴ ~E

    Name: Modus tollens   Valid: Yes

4. K ⊃ L   K = Paul did not know the Ephesians.
    L   L = Paul wrote them a letter.
    ∴ K

    Name: Affirming the consequent   Valid: No

✒ EXERCISE 35

Develop sound syllogisms which establish the given statements as conclusions, using the suggested mood and figure in parentheses.

1. Everyone in heaven is happy. (AAA-1)

> All glorified people are happy people.
> All people in heaven are glorified people.
> Therefore, all people in heaven are happy people.

2. Bats aren't bugs. (EAE-2)

> No bugs are mammals.
> All bats are mammals.
> Therefore, no bats are bugs.

3. Many spirits are demons. (IAI-3)

> Some angels are demons.
> All angels are spirits.
> Therefore, some spirits are demons.

4. Some people will not be saved. (EIO-2)

> No saved people are condemned people.
> Some people will be condemned people.
> Therefore, some people will not be saved people.

For the following problems, develop sound syllogisms which establish the given statements as conclusions, using whatever syllogism form you like.

5. Socrates is mortal.

>   All men are mortals.
>   All Socrates is a man.
>   Therefore, all Socrates is a mortal.

6. Whoever turns away from Christ cannot be his disciple.

>   All Christ's disciples are people who faithfully follow Christ.
>   No people who turn away are people who faithfully follow Christ.
>   Therefore, no people who turn away are Christ's disciples.

7. Some teachers are fathers.

>   Some pastors are fathers.
>   All pastors are teachers.
>   Therefore, some teachers are fathers.

8. Not all roads lead to Rome.

>   No American freeways are to-Rome leaders.
>   Some roads are American freeways.
>   Therefore, some roads are not to-Rome leaders.

9. Logic is an art.

> All activities involving creative skill are arts.
> All logic is an activity involving creative skill.
> Therefore, all logic is an art.

10. Some problems are not hard to solve.

> Some sums are not hard to solve problems.
> All sums are problems.
> Therefore, some problems are not hard to solve problems.

ANSWERS TO SELECTED UNIT 4 REVIEW EXERCISES

✒ *ADDITIONAL EXERCISES FOR LESSON 27*

1. The immediate inferences learned in this lesson are species of what genus? Expand the "Relationships Between Statements" genus and species chart to include *converse, obverse,* and *contrapositive.*

The immediate inferences in this lesson are species of equivalence forms. So the relationship between statements chart now expands to this:

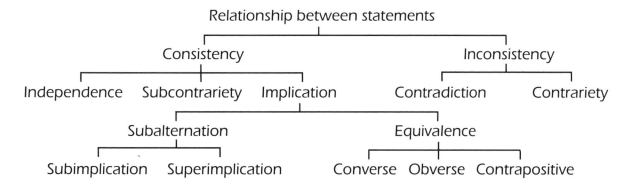

2. The converse is the only immediate inference which does not use the complement. What is unique about the obverse? the contrapositive?

Only the obverse keeps the subject and predicate in the same position.
Only the contrapositive changes the subject to its complement.

3. Give an example of a false E statement which has a true contrapositive.

No non-cats are mammals is a false E statement (for example, dogs are non-cats that are mammals). Its contrapositive is *No non-mammals are cats,* which is true (since all cats are mammals).

Write two equivalent immediate inferences for each of the following statements.

4. All exothermic reactions are energy releasers.

Obverse: No exothermic reactions are non-energy releasers.
Contrapositive: All non-energy releasers are non-exothermic reactions.

5. No large democracy is an effective government.

Obverse:	All large democracies are non-effective governments.
Converse:	No effective government is a large democracy.

6. Some pagan myths are profitable reading.

Obverse:	Some pagan myths are not non-profitable reading.
Converse:	Some profitable readings are pagan myths.

7. Some friendly neighbors are not Christians.

Obverse:	Some friendly neighbors are non-Christians.
Contrapositive:	Some non-Christians are not non-friendly neighbors.

8. All impossible events are improbable events.

Obverse:	No impossible events are probable events.
Contrapositive:	All probable events are possible events.

9. No penguins are non-swimmers.

Obverse:	All penguins are swimmers.
Converse:	No non-swimmers are penguins.

10. Some exercises are unhealthy activities.

Obverse:	Some exercises are not healthy activities.
Converse:	Some unhealthy activities are exercises.

11. Some defendants are not nonresponsive witnesses.

Obverse:	Some defendants are responsive witnesses.
Contrapositive:	Some responsive witnesses are not non-defendants.

Translate the following arguments into standard-form categorical syllogisms, and determine their validity.

12. No fantasy is non-fiction. Thus, much fiction is interesting stuff, for no uninteresting stuff is fantasy.

          All fantasy is interesting stuff.
          All fantasy is fiction.
∴ Some fiction is interesting stuff.   Valid

13. All non-Olets are progressive wardens, because all obstructionists are non-progressive wardens, and no Olets are non-obstructionists.

> All Olets are obstructionists.
> All obstructionists are non-progressive wardens.
> ∴ All non-progressive wardens are Olets.   Invalid

14. No dinosaurs were mammals, but most non-apatosaurs were non-mammals. Therefore, many dinosaurs were not apatosaurs.

> Some non-mammals were non-apatosaurs.
> All dinosaurs were non-mammals.
> ∴ Some dinosaurs were non-apatosaurs.   Invalid

15. Some good sleepers are non-pacifists, for snipers are never pacifists, but a few good sleepers are not non-snipers.

> No snipers are pacifists.
> Some good sleepers are snipers.
> ∴ Some good sleepers are not pacifists.   Valid

✎ ADDITIONAL EXERCISES FOR LESSON 28

Translate the following statements into standard categorical form.

1. Paris is beautiful in the springtime.

> All Paris in the springtime is a beautiful city.

2. Scotty is not a miracle worker.

> No Scotty is a miracle worker.

3. Elephant bellows can travel six miles.

> Some elephant bellows are six-mile travelers.

4. Gangsters do not obey the law of the land.

> No gangsters are law-of-the-land obeyers.

5. If Satan casts out Satan, then his kingdom cannot stand.

   No times Satan casts out Satan are times his kingdom can stand.

6. You could be a musician if you could make sounds loud or mellow.

   All loud or mellow sound makers are potential musicians.

Translate the following arguments into standard categorical syllogisms and determine their validity.

7. Toddlers never study calculus. So Sammy is not a calculus student, since he is still a toddler.

   No toddlers are calculus students.
   All Sammy is a toddler.
   ∴ No Sammy is a calculus student.   Valid

8. Some of the days in Genesis chapter one are not ordinary days, because ordinary days are caused by the sun, and not all of the days in Genesis chapter one were caused by the sun.

   All ordinary days are sun-caused days.
   Some Genesis-one days are not sun-caused days.
   ∴ Some Genesis-one days are not ordinary days.   Valid

9. Children were singing in the park, and anyone who sings in the park entertains me. Therefore, some children entertained me.

   All in-the-park singers are me-entertainers.
   Some children were in-the-park singers.
   ∴ Some children were me-entertainers.   Valid

10. If you don't have a brain then you can't talk. But the scarecrow could talk. So he must have had a brain.

   All people who can talk are people with a brain.
   All the scarecrow was a person who could talk.
   ∴ All the scarecrow was a person with a brain.   Valid

✒ ADDITIONAL EXERCISES FOR LESSON 29

Translate the following arguments into standard categorical syllogisms, and determine their validity.

1. Whatever is undeserved is unjust. Therefore, giving extra credit is not just, since giving extra credit is undeserved.

   > All undeserved actions are unjust actions.
   > All giving extra credit is an undeserved action.
   > ∴ All giving extra credit is an unjust action.   Valid

2. The boy squeals whenever he hears that song, and once during church he heard that song. So once during church he squealed.

   > All times he hears that song are times the boy squeals.
   > Some during church time was a time he heard that song.
   > ∴ Some during church time was a time the boy squealed.   Valid

3. Rocks are not food, because only food can be digested, and rocks are indigestible.

   > All digestible things are food.
   > No rocks are digestible things.
   > ∴ No rocks are food.   Invalid

4. The boys will dunk whoever gets too close to the pool. So some people won't get dunked, since some people won't get too close to the pool.

   > All close-to-the-pool people will be dunked people.
   > Some people will not be close-to-the-pool people.
   > ∴ Some people will not be dunked people.   Invalid

5. Allah is an idol, for anything that is worshiped is an idol except for the true God, and Allah is a false god that is worshiped.

   > All worshiped false gods are idols.
   > All Allah is a worshiped false god.
   > ∴ All Allah is an idol.   Valid

6. You may eat whichever piece you like. You would like the biggest piece. So you may eat the biggest piece.

> All the piece you like is a piece you may eat.
> All the biggest piece is the piece you like.
> ∴ All the biggest piece is a piece you may eat.   Valid

7. He wins the game unless he makes a mistake. Some times he doesn't make a mistake are still not perfect games. Thus, not every time he wins is a perfect game.

> Some non-mistake times are not perfect games.
> All non-mistake times are game winning times.
> ∴ Some game winning times are not perfect games.   Valid

8. This form of treachery shall never again endanger us, because this form of treachery we will always fight, and nothing we continue to fight will endanger us.

> No thing we fight will be a danger to us.
> All this form of treachery will be a thing we fight.
> ∴ No this form of treachery will be a danger to us.   Valid

✒ ADDITIONAL EXERCISES FOR LESSON 30

Translate the following enthymemes into standard categorical syllogisms. Put the assumed statement in parentheses (note that one of the enthymemes assumes the conclusion).

1. Enoch was not found, because God had translated him.

> (No God-translated person is a found person.)
> All Enoch was a God-translated person.
> ∴ No Enoch was a found person.

2. The Bible alone is God's Word. Therefore, the Book of Mormon is not God's Word.

> All God's Word is the Bible.
> (No Bible is the Book of Mormon.)
> ∴ No Book of Mormon is God's Word.

3. Anyone who claims to forgive sins is claiming to be God, and Jesus claimed to forgive sins.

> All people claiming to forgive sins are people claiming to be God.
> All Jesus was a person claiming to forgive sins.
> (∴ All Jesus was a person claiming to be God.)

4. Blessed are the meek, for they will inherit the earth.

> (All earth inheritors are blessed people.)
> All the meek are earth inheritors.
> ∴ All the meek are blessed people.

5. You are a teacher who has come from God, for no one could perform the miraculous signs you are doing if God were not with him.

> All miraculous sign performers are people who have come from God.
> (All you are a miraculous sign performer.)
> ∴ All you are a person who has come from God.

ADDITIONAL EXERCISES FOR LESSON 31

Consider this hypothetical statement: "If you heed instruction then you will prosper."
    I. What is the antecedent? What is the consequent?

> Antecedent: You heed instruction.
> Consequent: You will prosper.

2. Use this statement as the first premise to construct a modus ponens.

> If you heed instruction then you will prosper.
> You heed instruction.
> Therefore, you will prosper.

3. Use this statement as the first premise to construct a modus tollens.

> If you heed instruction then you will prosper.
> You do not prosper.
> Therefore, you do not heed instruction.

Identify the form of the following hypothetical syllogisms. Your options are *pure hypothetical syllogism (valid or invalid), modus ponens, modus tollens, affirming the consequent, denying the antecedent.*

4. If anyone is sick, then he should pray. Joseph is not sick, so Joseph does not need to pray.

    Denying the antecedent

5. If there is no vision, then the people perish. We must have no vision, for we are a perishing people.

    Affirming the consequent

6. Jesus said, "If you love me you will keep my commandments." John loves Jesus, therefore John keeps His commandments.

    Modus ponens

7. If you are predestined then you are called, and if you are called then you are justified. Thus, if you are predestined then you are justified.

    Pure hypothetical syllogism (valid)

8. If you trust in Christ then you are saved. Judas was not saved, so he must not have trusted in Christ.

    Modus tollens

9. If Jesus is John raised from the dead, then miraculous powers would be at work in Him. Miraculous powers are at work in Him. He must be John raised from the dead.

    Affirming the consequent

10. If he is the Antichrist, then he opposes God's people. If he is the Beast, then he opposes God's people. Therefore, if he is the Antichrist then he is the Beast.

    Pure hypothetical syllogism (invalid)

✒ ADDITIONAL EXERCISES FOR LESSON 32

Develop valid syllogisms which establish the given statements as conclusions.

1. A joke is a very serious thing.

> All different perspectives on things are very serious things.
> All jokes are different perspectives on things.
> ∴ All jokes are very serious things.

2. There is no one righteous, not even one.

> No sinner is a righteous person.
> All people are sinners.
> ∴ No person is a righteous person.

3. Some athletes earn straight A's.

> All Joe is a straight-A earner.
> All Joe is an athlete.
> ∴ Some athletes are straight-A earners.

4. Some earthquakes are not dangerous.

> No undetectable events are dangerous events.
> Some earthquakes are undetectable events.
> ∴ Some earthquakes are not dangerous events.

Imagine that you are preparing a debate over whether or not animals will be in heaven.

5. Develop two valid syllogisms with this conclusion: "Some animals will be in heaven."

> a. All resurrected creatures will be creatures in heaven.
>   Some animals will be resurrected creatures.
>   ∴ Some animals will be creatures in heaven.
> b. Some men will be creatures in heaven.
>   All men are animals.
>   ∴ Some animals will be creatures in heaven.

6. Develop two valid syllogisms with this conclusion: "No animals will be in heaven."

> a. No creatures in heaven are beasts.
>   All animals are beasts.
>   ∴ No animals will be creatures in heaven.
> b. All creatures in heaven will be creatures with souls.
>   No animals are creatures with souls.
>   ∴ No animals will be creatures in heaven.

UNIT FIVE

INFORMAL FALLACIES

CONTENTS

✒ EXERCISE 36

Identify the fallacy of distraction which is being made in each of the following examples.

1. Oswald must have been the lone assassin of Kennedy. Nobody has ever been able to prove any of the conspiracy theories.

   Ad ignorantiam

2. Santa Claus must be real. The editor of the newspaper said so.

   Ipse dixit

3. You believe in Jesus because you were brought up in a Christian home.

   Bulverism

4. We need to appropriate billions of dollars for AIDS research. Otherwise, you or someone in your family will probably get AIDS within the next ten years.

   Ad baculum

5. You don't believe that Genesis is to be understood *literally*, do you? That's a rather old-fashioned doctrine.

   Chronological snobbery

6. We should say the pledge of allegiance at our assemblies just like other schools do.

   Ad populum

7. A heretic named Servetus was burned at the stake in Geneva, and John Calvin approved of it. Calvinism has to be wrong.

   Ad hominem

8. You can't tell me it's wrong to cheat. You've cheated before too!

   Tu quoque

9. Do you disagree with me when I say that mankind is corrupt? That proves that you have been corrupted already.

    Ad hominem

10. The senator is accused of communist activities, and there is nothing to disprove these suspicions.

    Ad ignorantiam

11. You should read this book that your boss wrote. You would not want to jeopardize your position in this company, would you?

    Ad baculum

12. The vice-president said that potato is spelled with an "e" at the end, so it must be true.

    Ipse dixit

13. Professor Pepper thinks teachers should get paid more so they won't leave teaching for other jobs. But he's a teacher himself, so that figures.

    Bulverism

14. My dad tells me that I shouldn't shoplift, but I don't listen to him, because I happen to know that he stole candy from stores when he was a kid.

    Tu quoque

15. Of course God exists. Belief in a deity is one of the most ancient concepts of man.

    Chronological snobbery

✒ *EXERCISE 37*

Name the fallacies of ambiguity being made in the following examples.

1. Mother, you told me not to take any cookies. I didn't *take* them anywhere—I ate them right here.

   Accent

2. Super Frosted Sugar Bombs must be nutritious, because they are part of this nutritious breakfast.

   Division

3. My friend said that he hit his head on a rock, breaking it into a million pieces. But I don't think anyone could live with a shattered head!

   Amphiboly

4. Teacher: "I instructed you to write a letter to someone, and you haven't done it." Student: "Yes I did. I wrote the letter *A.*"

   Equivocation

5. Jesus taught that we should love our *neighbor.* So it's okay to hate the people across town.

   Accent

6. If two teaspoons of sugar make this taste good, then four will make it taste twice as good!

   Composition

7. Bread and water is better than nothing, but nothing is better than a steak dinner. So bread and water is better than a steak dinner.

   Equivocation

8. That was an expensive dinner. I wonder how much the water cost!

    Division

9. I read on the front page, "Grandmother of Eight Makes Hole in One." Her poor grand-child!

    Amphiboly

10. "Mary had a little lamb"? I'll bet the doctor was surprised.

    Equivocation

✒ EXERCISE 38

Identify the following fallacies of form by name.

1. My mom wouldn't take me to the movies, and she wouldn't let me watch a video. She never lets me have any fun!

   Apriorism

2. President Schwartz was just elected, and the stock market soared to new heights. I'm glad I voted for him.

   Post hoc ergo propter hoc

3. "Have you stopped getting drunk all the time?" "No!" "Oh, so you admit to being a drinker!"

   Complex question

4. Rotten Banana is a great band. I know, because all the cool kids like them. Which are the cool kids? The ones who like Rotten Banana, of course!

   Circular reasoning

5. That guy from the community church reads all the time. They must all be bookworms out there.

   Apriorism

6. If you leave the Christian school, then you will have to go to the public schools.

   Either/or

7. I didn't study because I had to go to church. I got an A on the test anyway. I'm going to go to church before tests more often!

   Post hoc ergo propter hoc

8. Miracles don't happen because that would violate natural law, and natural law cannot be violated.

    Circular reasoning

9. She killed the Wicked Witch of the East. So she must either be a good witch, or a bad witch.

    Either/or

10. Ever since I started eating seaweed with my meals, I haven't gotten sick once. You should eat it, too!

    Post hoc ergo propter hoc

✒ *EXERCISE 39*

Identify the fallacies made in the examples below. They can be any of the fallacies of distraction, ambiguity, or form.

1. The chain letter read, "If you don't keep this letter going, you may lose your job, get in an accident, or go bald!"

   Ad baculum

2. That chain letter was real! Just a week after I threw it away, I failed my logic test.

   Post hoc ergo propter hoc

3. My girlfriend always keeps chain letters going. She says that nobody has proven to her that they don't really work.

   Ad ignorantiam

4. A recycling poster said, "Recycle cans and waste paper," so I am wasting paper every chance I get!

   Amphiboly

5. All my friends recycle their cans, so it must be a good thing to do.

   Ad populum

6. I read that "Life is either a daring adventure, or nothing." My life certainly isn't a daring adventure, so I guess it's nothing.

   Either/or

7. The apostle Paul told us to honor our leaders. But he dishonored the high priest, so why should I listen to him?

   Tu quoque

8. Honoring your leaders is an old tradition that no longer applies to our modern, sophisticated age.

Chronological snobbery

9. The Japanese always score higher on math than the Americans. So I am sure our Japanese neighbor can help you with your calculus.

Division

10. The Japanese are better at math because they're smarter. We know that they're smarter, because they always do better at math.

Circular reasoning

11. Hi, I am selling tickets to the policemen's ball, and I am sure you would like to support your local police, so how much would you like to give?

Complex question

12. Of course the Joint-Chiefs-of-Staff say we ought to increase military spending. As members of the armed forces, they want as much as they can get.

Bulverism

13. We shouldn't listen to Senator Slug either, since we all know he is a card-carrying member of the radical right.

Ad hominem

14. Oh, so you believe in evolution? Tell me, are you descended from a monkey on your mother's side or your father's side?

Either/or, ad hominem

15. The world was not created by God, for matter has always existed, and thus needs no God to explain where it came from.

Circular reasoning

16. The press has a duty to publish what is clearly in the public interest. And there is certainly public interest in the private life of the rich and famous.

    Equivocation

17. I had a bad time with my former husband. Trust me, dear, men are no good.

    Apriorism

18. The idea of trying to colonize Mars is ridiculous. My mother said it couldn't possibly work.

    Ipse dixit

19. Each snowflake is very light. There is no way that snow could make that roof collapse.

    Composition

20. Did that last guy say that snowflakes were light? I always thought that snow was frozen water.

    Equivocation

Challenge: Find and identify some informal fallacies from books, newspaper articles, headlines, or even comic strips.

ANSWERS TO SELECTED UNIT 5 REVIEW EXERCISES

✎ ADDITIONAL EXERCISES FOR LESSON 33

1. Most of the fallacies of distraction appeal to some element of fear. Explain the form of fear being appealed to for each one.

> *Ipse dixit* appeals to the fear of authority; specifically, the fear of what will happen if you ignore or disagree with someone in authority.
> *Ad populum* appeals to the fear of going against the crowd, of somehow missing out, i.e. the fear of peer pressure.
> *Ad baculum* appeals to fear broadly, usually to the fear of pain.
> *Ad hominem* appeals to the fear of being labeled as a bad person, either directly, or by association with another bad person.
> *Bulverism* appeals to the fear of being considered a poor reasoner.
> *Tu quoque* appeals to the fear of being considered an inconsistent reasoner.
> *Ad ignorantiam* is not directly an appeal to fear, unless it is the fear of being thought of as a person who disbelieves something without good reason.
> *Chronological snobbery* appeals to the fear of being out of step with the times.

2. *Ipse dixit* is an illegitimate appeal to authority. What are the characteristics of a legitimate authority? Where do we as men derive true authority over other men?

> All true authority is derived from God, the ultimate authority. Scripture is a true authority as God's Word. God has also established four main human authorities: civil government, family government, church government, and self government. All true authorities, such as the authority of the local police or of your school teacher, are derived from these authorities. Other factors may come in as well: education (e.g., someone can be an "authority in his field"), moral authority, and so on.

3. The classic counterexample for *ad populum* is apparently learned by all mothers of teenagers. Give the classic response of a mother whose teenage child argues, "But mom, all my friends are doing it!"

> If all your friends were jumping off a cliff, would you jump off a cliff, too?

4. Find some characters in comic strips who regularly appeal *ad baculum.*

> Moe (in *Calvin and Hobbes*) and Lucy (in *Peanuts*) are two good examples.

5. Explain why World War II was not simply a massive example of *ad baculum.*

   The civil authorities of the Allied nations in WWII were legitimate authorities, and their goal was a proper one, broadly speaking.

6. How is *ad hominem* the counterpart to *ipse dixit?*

   Generally, *ipse dixit* follows the pattern "X says p, and X is good, so p must be true," while *ad hominem* generally follows the pattern "X says p, and X is bad, so p must be false."

7. Bulverism and *tu quoque* are often considered to be species of *ad hominem.* Explain why.

   Someone who commits *ad hominem* verbally attacks a person in general. With Bulverism, the attacker points out the person's source of belief, trying to make it appear that his source is insufficient. With *tu quoque,* the attacker points out the inconsistency between a person's words and his actions.

8. *Ad ignorantiam* is part of our legal system — someone is innocent if they have not been proven guilty. Does something like chronological snobbery operate in our legal system as well? Explain.

   The statute of limitations is something like a legal version of chronological snobbery. This statute assigns a certain time after which offenses can no longer be legally punished.

✒ ADDITIONAL EXERCISES FOR LESSON 34

1. What type of definition helps to avoid equivocation?

   A lexical definition, which gives a single, established meaning of a term.

2. How does equivocation relate to what you learned earlier about verbal disagreements?

   In both cases, two different definitions of a word are being used without everyone involved being aware of the fact.

3. A fallacy similar to equivocation may occur when people misinterpret completely different words which happen to sound the same. Give an example.

   Puns can be an example of this, such as "That dessert will just go to *waist.*"

4. Consider this fallacious argument: "The buffalo are disappearing. That creature is a buffalo, so it must be disappearing too!" How could this be considered a fallacy of equivocation? How could it be considered a fallacy of division? Which is the better answer, and why?

This could be considered an equivocation on the word "disappearing": first meaning "becoming less numerous," and second meaning "fading from view." It could be considered a fallacy of division because what is true of buffalo as a whole is not necessarily true of each individual buffalo. Equivocation is the better answer, however, because even considered as a fallacy of division, the word is taking on different meanings: Buffalo as a whole are becoming less numerous, but that doesn't mean that an individual buffalo is fading from view.

ADDITIONAL EXERCISES FOR LESSON 35

1. In one sense, circular reasoning is perfectly valid: obviously a statement follows from itself. Why, then, is circular reasoning considered a fallacy?

Because the conclusion is not established by other, more accepted premises. The problem is not that it is invalid, but that it is unhelpful.

2. What distinguishes apriorism from a legitimate generalization? Consider doing some additional study on inductive reasoning.

Apriorism considers too few instances to establish a strong conclusion. A good college-level logic text may have a section on induction.

ADDITIONAL EXERCISES FOR LESSON 36

1. This book does not include all the possible informal fallacies. What other fallacies exist? Consider doing some research to learn about other fallacies.

Other popular fallacies include *red herring* (an argument that distracts the audience from the real issue), *subjectivism* (arguing that something is true because one wants it to be true), *hypothesis contrary to fact* (arguing that, if an event had occurred differently in the past, a specific instance in the present would be different), and *false analogy*.

2. What is the value of learning how to identify informal fallacies? How should a Christian respond to someone whom they hear committing an informal fallacy?

One who can identify fallacies is less likely to be swayed by them in actual discourse, *and will be more prepared to explain why the reasoning is poor and to correct it. As Christians, we should learn the names of fallacies, not to tear people down, but to build them up. When you hear your neighbor committing a fallacy, your response should not be, "Ha! Ad hominem!" but rather, "Friend, that is not the best way to argue your point. Consider this..."*

3. Find the book *The Many Loves of Dobie Gillis* by Max Shulman, and read the short story "Love is a Fallacy." Which fallacies mentioned in that story are included in this text?

    The story discusses these fallacies: dicto simpliciter, <u>hasty generalization</u>, <u>post hoc</u>, contradictory premises, ad misericordiam, false analogy, hypothesis contrary to fact, poisoning the well. (Underlined fallacies are ones discussed in this text.)

Identify the following fallacies by name.

5. UFOs are either alien spaceships, or the delusions of a few crazy people looking for instant fame.

    Either/or

6. UFOs aren't alien spaceships. That idea went out of style with the *Star Trek* generation.

    Chronological snobbery

7. The advertisement read, "Dog for sale. Eats anything and is especially fond of children." Well, I sure won't buy *that* dog!

    Amphiboly

8. I am nobody. Nobody is perfect. Therefore, I am perfect.

    Equivocation

9. You're telling me that speeding is illegal? Well, how many speeding tickets do *you* have?

    Tu quoque

10. Mr. Jones says he is honest, so I believe him, since honest people don't lie.

    Circular reasoning

11. You can't believe anything Jones says. He's just a blue collar worker who doesn't even have a college diploma.

    Ad hominem

12. If taking a vitamin a day will help me to be healthy, I should take a whole bottle of vitamins to be really healthy!

    Composition

13. I don't need vitamins! You just think you should take vitamins because your father works in a drug store.

    Bulverism

14. Teacher: "The study of logic is valuable." Student: "Oh, so it's the *study* of logic that is valuable? That must mean that the practice of logic is a waste of time."

    Accent

15. Of course the study of logic is valuable. Schools all across the country are starting to teach logic.

    Ad populum

16. God does not exist. That philosophy professor said so, and he sounded like he knew what he was talking about.

    Ipse dixit

17. I don't think God exists either. Nobody has proven to me that he does.

    Ad ignorantiam

18. Let it be known at the outset of this biology class that I will not tolerate arguments seeking to support creationism. You do want to pass this class, don't you?

    Ad baculum

19. The archaeopteryx fossil is half bird, half dinosaur. This proves that all animals evolved from one species.

    Apriorism

20. Doctor: "Have you ever given up smoking?" Patient: "No, I haven't." Doctor: "Then I'll just write down that you are still a smoker."

    Complex question

21. Sandy must be rich. She lives in one of wealthiest sororities on campus.

    Division

22. Those are Sandy's lucky shoes. The last time she wore them she passed her logic test.

    Post hoc ergo propter hoc

23. Neighbor: "Your hog got into our garden again. You need to get him a pen." Farmer: "Why? He can't even write with a pencil!"

    Equivocation

24. Men must be basically good. I heard them sing a song about it on children's television.

    Ipse dixit

25. That sign said, "Use right shoulder to install chains." Why, that would take years!

    Amphiboly

26. Each pixel on the computer monitor is motionless. Obviously, the monitor cannot show motion.

    Composition

27. Politician: "Thus I have proven that all communist nations are allied with Russia." Reporter: "What about China? They aren't allied with Russia." Politician: "Really? Then they must not be true communists."

    Circular reasoning

28. My opponent says that abortion is murder, but 76% of the people disagree. He is clearly wrong.

    Ad populum

29. You can't believe what doctors tell you these days. They wear those ugly outfits, and most of them don't even sign their names legibly!

    Ad hominem

30. The televangelist said that if I didn't send any money to his ministry, I wouldn't be blessed by God. That's why I gave him so much.

    Ad baculum

31. That televangelist must have been right, because my uncle had a stroke less than a week after he refused to send him money.

    Post hoc ergo propter hoc

32. He thinks that the husband should be the head of the wife just because he is a man.

    Bulverism

33. Did you vote to increase money for food stamps, or do you prefer to let the poor starve?

    Either/or

34. "There are no mountain lions within a hundred miles of this city." "How do you know?" "Well, have you seen any?"

    Ad ignorantiam

35. The Old Testament law cannot be applied to society today. We need twenty-first century solutions to twenty-first century problems.

    Chronological snobbery